What people are say

Reason and Beyond

Darrell Morley Price herein offers a thought-full mixture of philosophical and spiritual wisdom for those seriously engaged in the discipline of self-knowing. Insightful lines of intellectual inquiry are blended with passages of poetic power to produce a handbook for self-study that will prove helpful both to the neophyte and the advanced learner. This is a book of uncommon clarity and usefulness.

The Reverend Michael J. Langlais, PhD, Pastor, Good Shepherd Lutheran Church, Norway, MI

You are about to read a powerful philosophical work examining exactly how your mind works, e.g. dealing with time, space and relativity. What makes it unique is that the philosophical prose is interspersed with sparkling poems that warm your heart, and all the while you are being guided to discover your True Self as expressed in this poetic passage: "Each of us must become in our own life a mountain peak that rises above what is meaningless and represents all that is best and highest in human life."

Raymond Comeau, PhD, author of *There Must Be Another Way: Reflections of a Mind Illuminated Through A Course In Miracles*, and *100 Haiku, Book Two: Inspired by the Mind Training of A Course in Miracles*

The clarity and experiential power of *Reason and Beyond* is like a fresh spring rain falling on a dry and parched world. The reader is gently led through a process of self examination, uncovering faulty reasoning, unconscious beliefs, and limiting ideas that interfere with our ability to be truly helpful and loving, qualities sorely needed in all our human relationships at this critical time.

We are here reminded that each of us shares in the responsibility to change the ideas in our own minds that are the source of the damaging and destructive influences in the world, and that each of us has the ability to do so. This book extends a helping hand, guiding us resolutely to a radical change in our own consciousness, which in turn supports the great transformational wave sweeping across the human mind as a whole in this present era of unprecedented change and uncertainty.

Leda Robertson, teacher of *A Course in Miracles*, co-author of *Reflections of Now*

Reason and Beyond

Knowledge, Belief and
Spiritual Transformation

Reason and Beyond

Knowledge, Belief and
Spiritual Transformation

Darrell Morley Price

BOOKS

Winchester, UK
Washington, USA

First published by O-Books, 2019
O-Books is an imprint of John Hunt Publishing Ltd., 3 East St., Alresford,
Hampshire SO24 9EE, UK
office1@jhpbooks.net
www.johnhuntpublishing.com
www.o-books.com

For distributor details and how to order please visit the 'Ordering' section on our website.

ISBN: 978 1 78904 097 5
978 1 78904 098 2 (ebook)
Library of Congress Control Number: 2018940332

A CIP catalogue record for this book is available from the British Library.

Design: Stuart Davies

UK: Printed and bound by CPI Group (UK) Ltd, Croydon, CR0 4YY
US: Printed and bound by Thomson Shore, 7300 West Joy Road, Dexter, MI 48130

We operate a distinctive and ethical publishing philosophy in
all areas of our business, from our global network of authors to
production and worldwide distribution.

Contents

Also by Darrell Morley Price:
From the Christ Mind (ISBN: 978-1-937748-01-2)
From the Christ Mind, Book II (ISBN: 978-1-937748-23-4)

The unexamined life is not worth living.
Socrates

Foreword

The concept of reason is used in these pages in a very specific way or context. I address very fundamental questions that relate to our modern way of life and thought and action by referring to certain basic facts that are obvious or can become so if you take the time to look or consider them; and then I draw seemingly obvious conclusions based on logical thinking in relation to these facts. My use of reason starts with the facts of the matter and always do I attempt to be aware of a priori assumptions, and use assumptions based on truth or human good. The reader can decide whether I have been successful or not in my attempts.

In a nutshell: I consider the thinking process to be guided by reason only if based on facts and/or on direct experience. And a conclusion is not reasonable unless it includes what is relevant, regardless of bias, as well as what is true. My conclusions have the goal of hopefully stimulating the reader to think about these issues carefully with an open mind. I have not the intention or the purpose, the desire or the right, to persuade or convince anyone. What you believe is your choice and your responsibility, and you will experience the consequences of your beliefs, of your thinking. Nothing more and nothing less.

Introduction

All human problems including the great ones we face in the modern era have their origin in the human mind. Our ways of thinking, self-understanding or the lack of it, values, judgments, biases, fears, perceptions, and beliefs, especially regarding the purpose and meaning of human life, shape and direct our lives both individually and on the world stage. As individuals, there may not be much that can be done directly to affect the great movements that determine history. Yet each of us can work on and influence for the better the origin of human culture and civilization, the human mind, our own human consciousness. We can make our own minds and our own lives part of the solution to what ails us and refuse to be part of the problem. The world is the result of the thoughts and actions of a great many people; it is here that each of us can begin to offer corrective thinking and action through our own lives, our relationships, our attitudes, and our feelings for each other, for Mother Earth and for all life.

In these pages, a way is presented by which we can align ourselves with Love, real understanding, and the Higher Power in which we all live and move and have our being, and thereby contribute towards the solution that is so needed. I hope the reader may join me in this if you are so inclined, and I hope what is contained in these pages may be helpful in some way. Many different themes are explored, yet all relate in some fashion to one central idea: I am part of the basic problem or part of the solution in everything I do, say, think, or feel, and the choice is mine every moment. Life takes place in the present; all problems begin and end there. From this fact comes our saving grace. Thank you for reading this book. May God bless us each and every one.

Chapter 1

Thinking

Almost all serious examination of the process of thinking and the acquiring of knowledge thereby is concerned with the data themselves, the contents of the process. Thoughts, feelings, reason, arguments, beliefs, these are endlessly examined, analyzed, dissected, compared and contrasted with each other. The questioning that drives philosophical inquiry, considered to be the most serious examination of what we know through our thinking process, is itself almost always limited to the content of thinking itself.

Much of what passes for thinking in our modern era is simply the exercise of the intellect within the boundaries of whatever paradigm has been accepted by the thinker. This is equally true of thinking on the greater scale of the many or in the mind of the individual. Thinking is used within narrow boundaries to confirm and reinforce what is already believed or used to defend those beliefs in argument with another.

Critical thinking is the examination of thinking itself. It is usually understood as the application of thinking to a particular argument or belief to ascertain the truth or falsity of it. I propose a more universal and self-examining type of critical thinking that looks at the process of thinking itself; not examining the products of thought such as beliefs, but at its own activity in the most basic way. Examining its process, from where it arises, and all the possible conscious and unconscious assumptions that inform it and the ignorance or unawareness that affects and conditions it.

First and foremost is the issue of awareness itself. All thinking takes place in awareness. Awareness is the most basic and fundamental aspect of what we call mind and somehow is usually overlooked. All thought, feeling, perceptions, impulses etc. arise in and take place in awareness. The whole process of thinking in all its details requires a subject who is aware of thought or there would be nothing happening. This subject is commonly regarded as identity, yet what is identity if not awareness? Through awareness you know your experiences, your perceptions, your likes and dislikes, joys and sorrows. If the sense of identity is not based on awareness then what is its foundation or core?

Let's begin with this assumption: The fundamental basis of identity is the essential and fundamental quality and aspect of mind that is awareness or consciousness itself. This awareness is aware that it is aware, i.e. it is self-aware. Self-awareness seems to be a fundamental part of awareness itself so perhaps we can say the sense of identity arises from the active experience of being aware of content that appears in awareness and experience, and the accompanying sense of being a self or aware entity in awareness to whom this content is appearing or to whom these experiences are happening. Actually, awareness is, in the most abstract sense, self-referentially aware without the need for an entity that seems to occupy it and to whom the content of experience is happening. However, we will leave this point for now and come back to it later.

Let's start with awareness itself as the individual experiences it and its relationship to critical thinking. I would suggest that to have a sound basis from which to exercise the faculty of critical thinking, an individual must be to some significant degree self-aware. That is, he/she must be quite familiar with their own mind, their beliefs, biases, limitations, likes and dislikes, history of judgments and the basis for them. The ability to think somewhat objectively must be a part of critical thinking. In order to have any chance of thinking objectively, you must be very honest with yourself and very aware of all the personal factors that affect and condition thinking and perception. Critical thinking in regard to any subject must be relatively free of bias, overt or covert. It is probably impossible to be completely free of subjective factors but it must be possible to be aware to a great degree of the presence of bias in one's mind, and, to the greatest degree possible, approach an issue clearly and honestly without allowing one's subjective factors to have an undue influence on thinking and the conclusions that may be drawn through careful examination. While it is true that all individual thinking is subjectively biased and greatly affected by one's belief system, to the degree that we can, in effect, step beyond that in the consideration of an issue, to that exact degree can the application of critical thinking be fair and capable of reaching a useful conclusion.

The day has been beautiful, a natural flow of events and experiences, each one effortlessly transforming into the next, a seamless movement of consciousness. Time is standing still; there is only one moment that is reborn again and again as the now. The present is ever with us, never is there a past or future that is directly experienced; always do they exist only as memory or imagination. And the past and the future are remembered or imagined only now.

Time is a very strange thing like a river that is motionless and yet constantly flowing. Always do we have the impression of movement within what is intangible, indefinable. It could be said that time is the measure of change; certainly it forms part of the background or context against which or in which change occurs. Yet what is time exactly? Supposedly it can be measured by our instruments in ever smaller and smaller intervals, but what is it exactly that we are measuring? Are not our time intervals completely arbitrary and simply imposed upon something we do not understand? In science, these intervals are used to measure change: Change of state, change of position, change of conditions, change of speed of movement against the background of space, and a host of other changes.

In the practical sense, perhaps we could say time is the "process" of change in the physical and mental factors that make up the superficial level of our experience. In a very basic sense we relate time to our planetary cycles: a day is one complete rotation of the earth on its axis; a year is one complete orbit of our planet around the sun. In both these cases the cycle of time we are measuring then repeats itself again for the next cycle and so on. Over a number of cycles or even less, we notice and measure change in the basic conditions around us. Light turns to dark then light again. The yearly cycle around the sun is marked by the change of seasons and the relative length of daylight and the darkness of night. Yet is there more to time than this?

Time is often experienced subjectively in different ways. The state of mind, the activity one is engaged in, the mood, even the conditions or circumstances, all these can seem to speed up time or slow it down or even "suspend" time for a short while. In classical physics, time, like space, was thought of as an inert, constant, unchanging background factor of existence. Einstein changed all that, demonstrating that as the speed of a body increases time slows down. When the speed of light is attained, time stops altogether.

It certainly seems as if time is not what we thought it was. Time is, in fact, in your mind as is everything else. Time and space are not separate. They are, as Einstein suggested, one thing indivisible: Time/space or space/time, arising together. To affect one is to affect the other. Here is an example: As you move through space at increasing speeds, time slows down for you. Your relationship with space, be it stationary or moving, affects the speed at which time moves for you. Without space, there is no change in time. Without time, there is no change in space. In fact time can be defined in a very basic way as the measure or medium of change occurring in space or in relation to a spatial reference. Without space there is no change in time for there is no measure of it. Without time, there is no change in space, for time is the medium of change.

Time and space arise together and inseparably. Every process that occurs in the physical universe is a change of form of some kind which is a part of space, and this change requires successive moments of time in which what is one thing or in one state becomes something else or changes its state into one with different characteristics. Change is inconceivable without time and space is inconceivable without form and process which undergo change thus requiring time.

So what is time then? And why do we hold moments of time long gone by in our memories? These memories are precious, often cherished, and may be with us for a lifetime. Why does time exist? To allow the process we call change? To provide, along with space with which it is inextricably wedded, an apparent backdrop against which change can occur and figures seem to move about? To obscure the unchangeable and unchanging Oneness that is everywhere the same? Time is a sleight of hand, a vast illusion we perpetuate upon ourselves for what apparent purpose?

Love is a very popular subject. So much has been written about it, so much attention given it almost to the point of obsession, it may seem as if everyone must understand what love is by now. You cannot be a member of our modern (or postmodern?) civilization without being barraged by an unceasing stream of visual media containing much material, many stories and presentations whose theme is wholly or partially "love." It may be love between human beings (and often is), love of family, romance, love of friends, of pets, of possessions and accomplishments. The romantic fixation in particular is an obsessive theme in so much of the entertainment material paraded before our eyes in many variations of the boy meets girl story, and despite the conflicts, difficulties, ambiguities, and contradictions often present as part of the story line, one question never seems to arise: Is the romantic fixation truly an expression of love?

What is Love? What is It really? Is It dependence, attachment, desire or attraction? Does It have anything to do with pleasure, security or comfort? Love Itself is a flame that burns brightly in the hearts of those who have given themselves to Love, who want nothing else but to be consumed by Love, giving up all else, all other attachments, laying them on the altar of Love until the whole world is reduced to ashes. When nothing remains but Love, when even the heart has been burned away leaving only emptiness, then Love will come to fill that emptiness and sorrow will be no more. Love embraces all, dissolving everything into Itself, leaving nothing to interfere or take Its place. Only then can freedom arise and loose the mind from the bonds of earth. Earth cannot hold the heart that rises on the wings of Love. Gravity cannot hold the mind that soars to the heavens propelled by the force that is Love. Love in Itself contains all happiness, all joy; all peace arises within It. How can gratitude and appreciation exist without Love? All that is good and right in the world, all kindness and generosity, charity and compassion, all high ideals whose purpose is the good of all have their source in Love. Love is a force, a mighty power for good, the power behind all true creativity for creativity is Love in action.

It has been said Love bears all, endures all, does not give way to pride or arrogance. Love forgives all; there is no act of hatred or violence that is not forgiven through Love. Love recognizes all are part of It. There are no exceptions and never will be. Only Love can heal all hurts, all conflicts, and make all things right again.

Whenever the urge to escape arises in your mind, what do you do? What are you escaping from? That is obviously the question to ask. What is it in your mind that you want to avoid? Could we say that fear is what you are trying to avoid? That's it, isn't it? The avoidance of fear is one of the main preoccupations of the human mind. Much of the behavior whose purpose is to avoid fear arises as an unconscious response; the individual may not be and often is not aware of the motivation that is driving action. Fear plays a major role in human life, not just the obvious fears around our relationships, vocation, money and achievements, but the more subtle psychological fears having to do with self-image, a sense of worth, the opinions of others etc.

The sunrise is behind me now as I head west, the sky brightening with the first light of dawn. This is the time of transition from the darkness and mystery of night to the clear and even harsh light of day, when everything begins to stand out in all its glory, its secrets revealed for all to see. The mind seems foggy, unclear, the subtle movements beneath its surface cloaked in invisibility, running their own course without any regard for what goes on above. So deep this thing called mind, its different levels seemingly pursuing their own aims and following their own laws, heedless of what goes on above or below. Yet every level affects all others and is affected by it in turn. Information filters down, is absorbed in different ways, digested or rejected, and its influence one way or another becomes part of the ongoing parade that is the constant movement of mind.

Whatever occurs to you must be filtered through mind and mind decides to act or not act according to past experience and tendency. Impulses that arise in consciousness are screened and evaluated, then judged good or bad, worthy or unworthy accordingly. Impulses from the deeper levels of mind are blocked and rejected, or recognized and welcomed. There is nothing that can enter your conscious mind without the willingness to receive it.

The mind thinks, "I am a body
I will live a little while
Then return to dust."
All bodies die, they were made
That they would die.
That is their purpose.

Mind ignores this fact,
Pretends death is far off, imaginary,
Until it comes knocking on the door.
"Go away," the mind says,
"I am not ready."
"That's what they all say," says death.
"You have forgotten our appointment,
It cannot be rescheduled,
You must come with me."
And go you will as the world
Vanishes before your eyes.
Death seems to be the enemy
Always with you.
A dark shadow,
Hidden in your mind,
Waiting, waiting,
For that appointed day.

Death has another purpose, a real purpose.
It reminds you to live and love,
It reminds you the world
Is not your home.
You are a visitor here,
An exile from a far country.
Death hands you a return ticket
To the world you left,
In the other hand is a free pass
Back to the land where
The sun never sets.
How you live here
Determines which you choose.

How could the wind do other
Than what it does?

Can a river refuse to return to the sea?
It can return now or wait
Thousands of years.
The ending will be the same.
For this it was created,
To flow, to flow until
The flowing becomes a silence,
The silence of the great ocean
That contains all.

Watch your mind, listen to it in silence. If you are patient and gentle, it will tell you about yourself, who you are and who you are not. Do this long enough and confusion will vanish. The mind will shine with a clarity that illuminates all things. But you must be patient, don't hurry it. All things come to those who wait. Mind cannot be forced to reveal itself. Let it show you what you are at its own pace, in its own time. Be quiet and observe today and tomorrow and the day after tomorrow and the day after that until today becomes tomorrow and the future is no more. Even today will vanish and you will disappear into awareness itself. Then nothing more can be said.

What am I?
Don't expect an answer.
Time was made for that question
Yet the answer is not in time.
Beyond all time is a place
Where all questions are answered,
Where the one answer to
All doubt, all questioning waits,
The mind cannot go where all words vanish.
Answer and question are the same wrapping.
Open the wrapping and nothing remains.
Live with that nothing.

Let it contain you and
You will know freedom.

Today is the day
Not tomorrow, yesterday,
Or the day after tomorrow.
The day is sufficient unto itself
Without recourse to what went before.
The future awaits your decision
To be what it will be.
Do not disappoint it, to cover it over
With the dust of the past,
Is to live in a graveyard
Before you are dead.

Do not turn and look
At what lies behind.
Empty mirages and phantoms.
Listen to the wind, let it guide you
To a place of refuge.
There is nothing else to do.
Let the branches all around you
Bend, each in its own direction.
Fly like an arrow to its mark,
Let nothing deter your silent flight.
If the eye of the archer remains true
Only the wind is heard rustling the pines.

Do not be afraid to be as nothing.
Somethings are afraid of everything.
Do not be a something.
At the core of everything is nothing.
Nothing thinks itself something
And form is born.

Time and space give shape to form.
They are but a stage upon which
Imagination invents experiences.
Experiences multiply, complexity appears,
Worlds wheel about within the chaos
Images in an empty mirror.
Hypnotized by sound and movement
You forget the mirror.
Mind is the mirror of emptiness.

The holy mountain stands aloof, unmoved by the activity below. Its blessings are given to all; its peace is freely bestowed upon those who are willing to share it. Nothing can disturb its majestic serenity, not even the noisy machines that race across the snow with their clatter and the stink of diesel fumes. The tiny creatures that crawl about on its slopes on two legs or four, come and go as the seasons change and the years pass away but the mountain remains, its presence beyond all change, all littleness. Once it arose as a great fire melted rock and ash sowing destruction, purging its slopes and the valley below of the past, of the growth of millennia. In time life returned, covering the charred ground with a carpet of green.

The summit, upraised, looked down on the changes it had wrought and found them good. And so it remains, waiting for the time when the fire will be called to return and cleanse the land below. For now, the mountain shares its beauty and silence with all and the life-giving waters flow to the valleys and villages that surround it. The Sacred Light of its Presence uplifts and heals hearts and minds and sometimes even bodies. No payment is asked; only the willingness to receive and to respect the power that gives itself so freely.

God has given his mountains a special purpose: to stand above the petty dramas and jealousies of human life, the endless conflicts and tragedy; to be images of beauty and strength that reach from the earth to the heavens, unaffected by change and human destiny. The mountains represent what we must strive for, what the great ones in our history have embodied. Each of us must become in our own life a mountain peak that rises above what is meaningless and represents all that is best and highest in human life. Each of us must become a place of beauty and healing, a source of the life-giving waters that flow into the pain and sadness of human life.

Some days seem strange, as if the minutes get out of step and begin to trip over one another. Things don't work out, there is no smoothness to activity; fits and starts, stumbles, and always the timing is wrong. Time is like an escalator that is breaking down and starting again. If you hold on long enough you will get to the top but you fall on your face when you get there. Before you stand on another escalator, so gingerly you step aboard holding tightly to the railing. Before you know it the day is over, the ride shuts down and it's time to sleep. Tomorrow is another day.

Nothing is stranger than time. No one knows what it really is yet all are in it, carried along helplessly it seems to some destination we know not where. It does no good to complain, you will go along for the ride whether you like it or not. Somewhere up ahead lies the future, glittering with promise, yet you can't get there from here. Instead the future comes to you disguised as today, a today that becomes yesterday, a memory of what was and will be again. The future has already happened though we don't remember until it gets here.

Time is very subtle; we cannot see it or grasp it but cannot deny its existence. The evidence of it is everywhere in the changes around us. How did this all happen we cannot say; it just does somehow. Over time the body changes; it grows up, matures, then slowly weakens. We have no control over time but we can try to control or mitigate its effects. Never are we more than partially successful for time is all-powerful and takes us where it will. "Time waits for no man" it is said and it waits for no woman either. All are swept along in the ceaseless flow that is time as it winds its way along towards the great ocean of eternity.

There is nothing static about time. As a child, I once tried to stop time by counting to three and then willing the present moment to hold still so I could grasp it but it would not hold still. I tried again, over and over until I realized life was not a static thing that could be grasped but rather something active, something that flowed without ceasing, carrying me along whether I wanted to go or not. At best we can seem to direct our lives, to control certain of life's conditions. Some are very good at this. Yet ultimately all control is lost when the sands of time have all poured through the narrow opening at the bottom of the hourglass carrying us with them as time empties itself into eternity.

Whatever time is lost
Cannot be found again
No matter where you look.
Fortunately, as my friend used to say,
"When God made time, He made plenty of it."
Yet is there only so much
Allotted to each of us.
Use it well.
You will not pass this way again.

The sun rises, trees bend with the wind,
My shadow falls across the wall.
It follows me everywhere I go
But vanishes when night comes.
The moon casts no shadows
They cannot live in reflected light.
We are like the moon,
We live by the reflected light

Of the Great Sun.
Live in that Light
All shadows will vanish.
The body is little more than a shadow
Lying across the face of the inner Sun.

* * *

The pines stand so straight and tall
The earth beneath them covered with needles.
Sunlight filters through the trees
Patches of light everywhere.
I sit in silence
Listening to the conversation of leaves
Dancing in the wind.
Birds telling their story
To each other and to me.
I'm amazed at what I hear.
The same story is told
A hundred different ways.
Joy then pain then joy again
Love and hate and love again.
Gain and loss and gain and loss,
Always the story repeats but the characters change.
The movements are different, situations alternate
Yet the result is always the same.

Whatever I say, it nevertheless seems to be wrong, incomplete or insufficient somehow; words fail me however I attempt to describe it. The Lord comes as He will and I have nothing to do with it other than to be receptive, willing, and aware; to be available to remember, to recognize in my heart and mind what I am being given, which is always something of His Presence, His Light, and His Love. Though this is very healing, lifting me out of the world for a time, it seems to uncover again and again another layer of darkness, of fear, anger and judgment, which must then be faced, understood, and healed. There seems to be no step forward without a requirement that more of the deeper layers of mind be exposed and the imperfections and resistances therein be purged. This purification of mind is an ongoing process that accompanies the whole movement of spiritual realization, also called spiritual awakening. The awakening of the lower nature, which is temporal and illusory to the higher nature by whose reflected light it is aware and to which it owes its existence, is an intense process that must take place on all levels of mind, being, and action. There is no progress, without the purgation of the mind for mind must become empty, clear, and undistorted in order to receive the reflection of Truth, of God, of His Light and Love.

Heaven cannot be taken by storm; all is given by grace. By grace we live and by grace we are released. Our part is to make ourselves available to that grace. This means a quiet, empty, and purified mind, and an open and surrendered heart. When all the activity of mind, the many thoughts, desires, and impulses are stilled, replaced by the desire for God, and all the attachments and affections of the heart dissolve into the Love for God, then God will come into that mind and heart. He has always been there but His Presence is covered over by the chaos of the human mind, its constant activity, and the divided allegiance of the human heart.

Whenever He wills, He will come but you must be ready. A clean and empty place must be made for Him within you for He cannot come into the midst of chaos and conflict. God will do His part and we must do ours. It takes great energy, strength of mind, and stability of attention to receive That which comes from far beyond the body and mind. The human mind, split by many contrasting desires and impulses, riven by divisions and contradictions, is too weak and scattered to receive much less hold the reflected Image of the Divine in the mirror of its Soul. Just as the moon is not reflected on the restless and stormy surface of the sea, so is God's Presence unable to register on the restless and turbulent mind filled by an unceasing parade of thoughts and restless emotions. You cannot have it both ways; either your mind and perceptions are turned to the things of this world, of the senses, or the mind, turned inward and stilled, sinks into the depths within where, in deepest peace and silence, it comes into communion with its Source.

What to do on a cold and rainy day?
Dress warmly, walk upon the mountain.
The forest always welcomes rain
The trees and shrubs delight in it.
Healing manna bringing life to a thirsty world.

Smell of damp pine needles,
Ravines filled again with the song
Of flowing water.
The drip drip drip from
The outstretched branches.
Joy cannot be measured
Yet it can be felt.
Cold gray sky, rain threatens,
The wind in the pines is still
Smell of damp earth.
Mind still, waiting for rain
I sit beside the flowing water
Emptiness all around,
Immeasurable fullness of Being.

There is no merit in doing what you must. That is done by all. To do what is necessary is easy. The pressure of necessity provides the motivation; little is asked of you. To do what is right is quite another matter. All too often right action or response is not convenient, does not benefit us only. Right action is seldom limited by self-interest nor is that its purpose. Right action benefits all, benefits the whole. That whole may be a group, a town, a family, the earth, or the web of life. Right action may have unforeseen consequences, consequences that extend into the future or beyond the immediately visible. Always it arises from Love, from the recognition that all are connected and all are affected by what each of us may or may not do. Right action rests on responsibility, the individual responsibility each of us has for those around us, for the life that surrounds us. Right action is always helpful and always necessary. Integrity is the capacity to act in harmony with the needs of all, to act without selfishness or narrow self-interest; even at times to undertake action that will seem to go against our self-interest. Integrity is rooted in the spiritual understanding that I am my brother's keeper, therefore I am called upon to love my neighbor as myself and everyone, without exception, is my neighbor.

It's been raining for two days. Low, dark clouds, grayness everywhere. The rain has been steady but not heavy, unceasingly pelting us from above. Cars of many different colors darting everywhere. The rain does not slow them down anymore. So important to get to where I am going as fast as possible regardless of consequences. Seems as if a sense of perspective, a rational valuation of tasks, of what I do and how I do it, has somehow vanished into the digital haze that hangs over so many minds. So much stimulation, so many apps to take the place of what I used to do myself, so many ways to avoid the present, the here and now, by turning my attention elsewhere. Meeting and experiencing life directly has lost its popularity, dethroned by a virtual "reality" that offers endless distractions. Many of us are becoming digital dunces, sitting in a little corner of our own minds, wondering who to text next or tweeting madly our latest banal thoughts to the world out there that we are so busy avoiding direct contact with.

Tweety birds tweet, humans converse, engage in meaningful communication, or so it used to be. We were made for better things; at least that's the way it seems to some of us. To spend so much of daily life staring at the little screen in your hands while the richness and beauty of life passes you by unnoticed is a great tragedy. When you see a beautiful sunset or mountain range, enjoy it, engage with it in your heart and mind, be present with it. Simply capturing it on your digital device is meaningless. To reduce life to a series of texts, tweets, and snapshots is to miss it entirely. And saddest of all is the fact that so few even notice what their life has become or remember when a little more sanity and perspective was a part of how we lived.

Do you know the name of the person(s) who live(s) next to you or across the street? Do you greet each other if your paths cross somewhere? Is there a sense of neighborhood where you live; is it a place where you can borrow a cup of sugar or a tire iron if the need should arise? Neighborhoods seem to be going out of fashion in many places, replaced by communities of strangers who have minimal contact with each other. What kind of life is it to live in isolation, in a kind of digital and emotional cocoon, a cocoon that does not allow its inhabitants to ever break out and find a sense of freedom. Humans are social beings. Throughout our history we have lived together and depended on each other for support in many ways. The increasing isolation from each other and from the simplicity of every day interaction with our fellow human beings seems to be gaining speed. The proliferation of substitutes for personal interaction such as e-mail and the various forms of social media seems almost like an unconscious attempt to fill in the growing void in human life. Yet these means are not the equal of what they replace but simply increase the distance between us. There is a place and a function for them. A sense of community via digital communication is better than no community at all but there is no adequate replacement for what we are losing. As society "progresses" and "evolves," there are tradeoffs always, and some things are lost or given up in order to gain what is considered of greater value. We have now reached a point, however, where the tradeoffs are becoming a bad deal. What is given up is too often significantly more valuable than what is replacing it though many do not seem to notice that as of yet. The obsession with ever new "toys" and gadgets seems to be reducing many of us to virtual children or perpetual adolescents always looking for new distractions or stimulations to keep us occupied.

Is reason sufficient to explain all our activities, the attitudes we hold and the values we embrace? Even a cursory look at the world situation, the conflict, fear, violence, and unrestrained greed that drive much of human life, makes apparent that often reason is absent in our day to day affairs, our relationships one with another, our values, and even our thoughts, words, and deeds. The ever-present tension and frantic busyness that drive us make peace and happiness seemingly impossible.

Have things ever been different in human life? Has a relative or sufficient degree of peace and harmony prevailed on the many levels on which human interaction takes place? There is, in some cultures at least, a recurring myth of a Golden Age in which just rulers led a peaceful and happy society based on the highest principles discovered by the human mind. Even now, our Western democratic society has attempted and continues this attempt to establish conditions under which the majority of citizens have a reasonable chance to pursue the good life: A sufficient measure of personal liberty, and individual happiness and fulfillment. The American concept of the "golden years" is perhaps a faint echo of the older myth reduced to the level of the individual, although in truth, the concept seems more of a marketing slogan held out like a carrot before the hardworking masses to keep their attention diverted from the present.

Consider the idea of a peaceful, harmonious existence in which happiness and contentment are attainable. Is not this a question of balance, a balance based on our understanding of the factors of life, of the underlying basis of life, and right relationship to each other, to the earth on which we live, and to the means by which we make a living and fulfill our needs and desires? I think it's safe to say that most every one of us, underneath the goals and activities of our lives, are seeking a sense of happiness and contentment, a happiness and contentment that we believe is dependent on our activities and the attainment of our goals whatever they may be.

Do not let your ignorance of your own Self continue to blind you to the Truth and the freedom that are part of you. You will not find happiness and harmony while you continue to chase ephemeral goals, goals without meaning, and ignore the only goal worthy of attainment. All the various activities, the frantic pursuits, the constant busyness of mind and body have the purpose of keeping you in a state of ignorance of what you truly are. This ignorance can be rectified but it requires your cooperation, interest, and willingness expressed as intent. Only when the realization of Truth becomes the single and central purpose of your life, on which it is based or around which it revolves, can the veil of ignorance be lifted that the Truth in your mind be revealed...

All day the wind has been blowing without ceasing, driving the rain clouds across the sky. At times they lift for a moment, revealing the blue sky above, then close up again. Coming close to the earth, they veil the forest in a gray shroud of fog. The rain has been furious, beating on the roof as if it would wash everything away. Finally, in the evening, exhausted by its effort, the rain became a gentle patter, blessing the thirsty earth. You can almost hear the trees rejoicing for there has been insufficient rain for several years now. Many trees have died or are dying. The survivors, the healthy and the weakened, are accepting their reprieve with gratitude as they stretch their limbs skyward to receive.

It would be good for us to follow their example, to give thanks for the blessings that rain upon us from above for we too are thirsty and dying. In the wasteland that modern life has become, the constant pursuit of nothingness disguised as attractive somethingness exhausts the mind and dulls the spirit. This may be done for an entire lifetime, postponing the reckoning for as long as possible, yet is meaninglessness still meaningless no matter how attractive the wrappings. And only death will be its reward for death has walked beside you unrecognized and patient, waiting for its appointed hour. To choose what is meaningless in place of Truth is a choice for death, not life. Whether you are aware of your choice or not, you will reap the consequences. Choices determine the direction of life and its details. It is not what you think you are choosing that is your reward, but the actuality of your choice that results in the consequences you will experience. In a state of ignorance about what is truly valuable and what is worthless, the shiny baubles so beloved of the ego dominate attention and often determine choices. Disneyland may seem like fun for a little while but behind the glitzy façade is nothingness.

The night is still, just the hiss of the gas heater and the sound of water dripping onto the roof from the trees. Alone in the little cabin on the side of the hill, the front of the cabin hanging over the precipice, held up by four beams like wooden legs poised to run away carrying me with them to some unknown destination, I rest in silence. The deep silence of the Self can be heard, can be felt. You can live in that Silence beyond thought, beyond the noise and chaos of the surface world. If you can abide there long enough, everything will disappear leaving only Silence aware of Itself.

There is a depth in the mind where thought cannot go nor can you for you are the result of your thoughts and cannot go beyond them. In that depth of mind lies a mystery, concealed from all the mind's surface activity, waiting for you to come in silence with empty hands and open heart.

Do you understand what you do and why you are doing it, what you think and why you think it? It is easy to get the impression that at times, even frequently, many of us are not truly aware of what we do or why. Can it fairly be said that much human activity is mechanical, repetitive, uncreative? If you or I are functioning in a drone-like manner, simply carrying out tasks by habit, tasks which your life requires or which are assigned by the business or social hierarchies, can meaning be found in what we are doing? The human mind clearly has a tendency to operate from past learning or conditioning. Action arising on that basis will always be habitual, mechanical. It cannot be otherwise for spontaneity, creativity, and the actual enjoyment of what we do are always of the present and the present is always new, fresh. The freshness, the originality of the present moment, assures that experience will not be a stale repetition of what has gone before. In order for this new, alive quality to be a part of your awareness, you must be vividly present with all your mind, free from the deadening influence of habit, of the past. The mind, and the eyes through which it sees cannot be dull, weighed down by yesterday's experience, by what has gone before. A mind weighed down by the past, carrying the heavy load of past events and experiences becomes deadened over time, repetitive, incapable of true spontaneity or creative response to the demands of the present.

Why is the human mind so prone to the conditioning of past experience and the influences around it? Could it be simply the need to function in habit, in routine, in a kind of groove that feels safe? Does this way of living and acting give us a sense of security, of regularity, that seems to reduce the insecurity of human life and protect us from life's inevitable changes?

As a lifelong observer of the human mind both from within and without, it seems to be an obvious fact that the mind itself is driven, consciously and unconsciously, by two competing desires: The desire for security, for safety, and the drive towards freedom and creativity. Creativity and freedom are always, at least to some degree, fellow travellers. And freedom and security are never on the same bus for they point in exactly opposite directions.

The drive for security has its roots in the earth and its tendrils in the mind. Security is the great obsession and goal of modern Western society; financial security, physical security, emotional security, and the security of good health. It would not be an exaggeration to say that a tremendous amount of effort and energy is utilized to attain and maintain the requisite degree of security deemed necessary by individuals and society as a whole. Undeniably a certain amount of security, call it freedom from want regarding basic needs such as food, clothing, shelter, healthcare, and personal safety, is desirable and necessary to maintain quality of life for the individual and the society at large. However, the fulfillment of basic needs is one thing and the embellishment of them with constant expansion and the invention of new "needs" or new variations on the basics is quite another.

The contrast or conflict between a choice for freedom and a choice for security does not revolve around the fulfillment of basic human needs. One need not be living in poverty and starving to turn one's life in the direction of freedom though that may be true for some. The issue is really one of degree. There are some who have found a measure of both freedom and security and there are those who are fixated on security alone with no thought of freedom. To lead a happy and balanced life, one needs both.

In human life you may often find situations in which you are seemingly called to choose between one or the other. The person drawn to artistic expression, the individual driven by the inner need to find a fulfillment that is not part of the normal routine of life, the loner seeking a freedom of life and soul not evident along the well-beaten path trod by the majority; all these must seek freedom not by degrees but as a way of life minimally compromised by the security motive. Such individuals must walk the road less travelled no matter where it leads. The mystic, the serious artist, the misfit who cannot conform to society's rules and norms; these are the ones who attempt to scale the heights of freedom, sometimes with success, sometimes to crash and burn like a shooting star falling to earth after its long journey across the heavens.

A mind dulled by conformity, carrying the heavy load of its past learning, its eyes ever looking downward, cannot be free, free to love, to learn. Dullness breeds more dullness, its steps are heavy and slow; it cannot catch up with freedom, with the new. Only a mind not tethered to the past has the quickness and openness to fully meet the present and embrace what it offers. In the naked present, you meet life directly. Life takes place in the present, the only moment of time that is directly available to experience. The need for security and sameness, for the safety and consistency found in habit, robs you of the present, covering it over with the memories of yesterday. You cannot see through the thick fog of concepts you carry from the past. Bringing the past to the present obscures it and renders it unreachable. You can't get here from there. A fresh start, a quiet mind, open and receptive, ready to learn, rests in the present and effortlessly receives what the present offers.

The wind is strong and steady tonight. At times it shakes the cabin; you can hear the sheet of canvas that covers the roof flapping like a sail trying to free itself from its moorings. Wind itself has a personality, sometimes gentle, playful, then teasing as it leaves to come back again a minute later. Tonight, however, it is very serious, shaking the tall pines as they sway slowly back and forth. Sometimes it roars, increasing in intensity until it tires of its sport. For a moment quietness, then gradually it comes back as if from afar, drawing closer and closer until it slams into the cabin with full force shaking the walls.

If the wind could talk, what would it tell us? Would it speak of places it has been, the havoc it may have wreaked, or of its home at the end of the world where all things begin, where all things are new? Does the wind ever get tired or wonder why am I doing this? Does it question its purpose or motives or does it leave those questions to others, letting them assign motive or purpose to what it does. Often the wind comes to greet me like an old friend when I step outside to look at the sky or thank the trees that provide the shade for my life. The wind and the trees have a mutually affectionate relationship. The wind enjoys rocking the trees and blowing loose the dead leaves and branches leaving them scattered across the forest floor. The trees enjoy their rocking motion as the wind blows through their branches. The only power of movement they have is the gift of brother wind.

What determines the worth of an individual human being? Is it the size of his bank account, the possessions he calls his own, his accomplishments in some arena of human life be it art, industry, politics or service? Can our worth be measured by the influence we wield in some way or the degree of public exposure we call fame? Is one human being worth more than another because he has accumulated more toys, more wealth? Or because one has a talent or skill that not many have, does that make him more valuable in some sense than the many who lack comparable talents? Is someone of high intelligence, as measured by a widely accepted standard, worth more than individuals of average intelligence? In what does the worth of a human being consist? Can we determine our worth by some universal standard or is it always a relative measurement related to time, place, and circumstance? Is the same individual with a certain mix of talent and influence worth more in one era than in another? Or is there a universal standard applicable to all at all times and in all circumstances; call it an intrinsic quality inherent in being human?

If there is a universal factor by which all can be evaluated, does it arise from the shifting and unstable judgments of the human mind or must it have its origin in a higher place? The Creator, the Intelligence, Power, and Love that has created us as we truly are, is the only authority capable of knowing and assigning worth to Its creation. To believe anything else is folly, arrogance based on ignorance. Only God knows the full value of all His creation, of every one of us. He has given of Himself in the act of creation, thus we live, move, and have our being in Him. We are literally part of Him, containing His Love and Beauty as part of our very being.

In the most fundamental and truest sense possible, we are, each and every one of us, of inestimable worth and value and no one stands higher than another in the sight of God. There is a Unity in which all inhere. From that Unity arises our very Being, and life. Each is a whole part of the Unity that is; each contains and is contained in the Whole. In this most fundamental and all-inclusive level of our existence, the very Reality of our existence, none is greater or of more value and worth than any other. The differences that are apparent on the level of time and space are temporary, and are a necessary part of the journey through time and space. They will disappear when the journey reaches its appointed end. Until then, our differences will be part of our expression here, and the proper use of all talents and abilities is to serve our fellow beings and the Great Plan of our Creator. Our talents and the success we enjoy through their utilization are not meant to be a source of pride or egoic self-justification but rather a reason to be grateful to God and to our brothers in whose service they are rightfully employed. Always there is a choice between God and the ego, Love and selfishness. Selfishness, the focus and preoccupation on our interests alone, often at the expense of others, will never lead to happiness or fulfillment.

Only Love, whose expression is giving and sharing, will bring the happiness and peace we seek.

Whatever is to be gained by your efforts on behalf of "others," the credit and the glory belong to God Who is the Source of your life, your mind, and the talents you seemingly possess. The Spirit and the Love within us is the doer and what is done. What we "do" for others is done for ourselves as well for giving and receiving are one in Truth. Whatever I give in Love will come back to me multiplied, maybe in a different form yet will it be the form that is needed. Spiritual Law has no exceptions. Whatever I give, I give to myself. This is one of the principles that rules life, and is the inner meaning of the Golden Rule. "Do unto others as you would have them do unto you" can also be expressed as give unto others what you would have them give unto you, i.e. give others what you would yourself receive because by giving it you are receiving it.

The forest stands silent, waiting for I know not what; always the trees, tall, straight, and silent, like parishioners in some vast, outdoor cathedral. They seem to communicate with one another gently, in silence, through a language unknown to us. The forest's moods change with the seasons and with the weather. Sunny, warm days bring relaxation, a gentleness that pervades all; a sleepy contentedness marks the trees, pine and leafy tree alike, as they gratefully drink in the sun's life-giving rays. By nightfall they come alive again, silent sentinels reaching to the sky, gracious in their presence. I feel them watching over me as I sleep, wrapped in profound silence like the softest of blankets. The bliss of Being permeates the welcoming darkness and all limitations fall away. The forest and I, one living, breathing aliveness, identityless, resting in the Ocean of Being that is God.

For now, we see through a glass, darkly; but then face to face.
Now I know in part; but then shall I know, even as I am known.
The Apostle Paul

Chapter 2

Myth and Reality

Myths drive the popular imagination and they become beliefs around which a persistent structure of related beliefs can develop or they can, of themselves, be the origin of further beliefs. Their function is to stimulate, arouse, or direct thinking and the associated emotions. Myths can even be said to be part of the foundation upon which empires and civilizations are built. They may serve as a unifying force, providing the justification and even the direction along which a human collective may pursue its destiny.

In the modern materialistic age, it is generally supposed that myths are something from a long ago and dimly remembered past, anachronisms that have been left behind, thrown onto the dust pile of quaint, ancient ideas and superstitions. The modern age has no use for them, nor will it allow itself to be limited by such antiquated nonsense, or so we think. We prefer to limit ourselves by our fascination with shiny, modern nonsense which, in characteristic fashion, we refuse to recognize for what it is. Yet much of modern life and thinking is dominated by conscious and unconscious allegiance to what can only be characterized as myths, ideas about the nature of reality, about how life should be lived and why. These modern ideas in themselves share the fundamental characteristics of the myth, though clothed in modern form, and have the same powerful effects on the emotions and thought processes and thus life itself. In that sense, life today is not all that different from life in ancient Rome or in medieval times despite our indulgence in the belief of our superiority.

Myth is defined as: A fiction or half-truth, a fictitious story or thing, or a story of a hero who serves as a primordial type, a

31

model of human behavior in the world view of a people. Here I would like to examine seriously some of the central elements of modern thinking, beliefs, and ideals that so resemble myths in their nature, use, and effects that to describe them in this way is nothing less than accurate. To use a more generalized terminology, all societies have certain "ideals" that they claim to follow or base society on, and which also frequently serve as models of proper human behavior. Some of these ideals in what they represent and the role they play in human life can also, on the basis of their nature, be characterized as myths.

Perhaps human thinking, no matter the time or place, ancient or modern, in the generalized sense always requires recourse to mythic or idealized concepts or stories to give it a base which supersedes the monotony and smallness of everyday life and provides a greater purpose or justification or picture of existence. Whether in terms of the transcendental or limited to the narrow confines of human bodily existence, this paradigm must provide a purpose or direction for life, however that is supposed, that serves to lift it above the ennui and repetition of the practical details of living and provides meaning or at least the justification for action.

What makes a mind "modern" is not just the time period in which it finds itself but the series of values, attitudes, and judgments about life and how it should be lived that it holds. When you look at all these factors and their expression in the form of culture, two features of the modern mind immediately stand out: The extreme self-centeredness that characterizes the individual, and the pervasive uncertainty or indifference about the meaning of life and its purpose. The thoroughly modern thinkers consider self-centeredness a very good thing. Here I am reminded of the enlightened self-interest that supposedly guides the economic marketplace, the activity of commerce, in such a way as to maximize the good of all. This is the idea proposed by Adam Smith that is the central justification for free markets and the modern economic philosophy of capitalism. It is certainly a fact that without regarding self-centeredness as a virtue, those who have amassed great wealth and become famous would not be regarded as heroes or role models to emulate. In past ages, the heroes have usually been those who through courage and virtue exercised for the good of the people, performed heroic acts for the good of all. Self-sacrifice has always been an element of heroic virtue.

In our modern mythology, however, our heroes, the primordial type of human that gives us a model for our human behavior, are very likely to lack completely the element of self-sacrifice or unselfishness, replacing it instead with an example of extreme selfishness in the pursuit of self-interest. They are admired and glorified and emulated for it.

Insofar as all societies are based to some extent on cooperation, though individual self-interest is never absent, self-interest must always to a degree be controlled or sacrificed for the good of the whole. The good of the whole is recognized as also good for the individual in certain respects; otherwise individuals would not consent to sacrifice their individual interest or agree to let boundaries be placed to limit its pursuit in certain fundamental ways. This is done through laws, political authority, norms etc., and enforced by penalties and punishments of various kinds administered by civil authorities. Always there exists in organized societies of any kind a continuing tension capable of becoming conflict between the naked and unconfined expression of self-interest and the governing authorities who must limit and regulate it to maintain social cohesion.

In modern society at the present time, this potential conflict takes many different forms. Some are obvious such as crimes against persons or property, and some are hidden, subtle, and relatively speaking, beyond the law as the self-interest in question may be shielded and protected legally though its result is detrimental to the greater society. This unequal and inconsistent application of limits on the exercise of self-interest is nowhere more self-evident than in the economic sphere and this is nothing new. Wealth has always meant power in the political sense and that power has always been exercised to protect the interests of the few, even if it conflicts with the interests of the many.

Here is the intersection of myth, control, and self-interest. To that I would add greed as a particularly potent expression of self-interest that at the present time has very far-reaching consequences for human society and our planetary home. Human greed and the extreme selfishness that can be part of it has often had drastic effects on large groups of human beings (think slavery) or on the environment (think the destruction of the famous cedars of Lebanon by the Ottoman Empire or the destruction of many other forests). This is a historical fact that cannot be denied, for the legacy of past greed on a large scale is with us today as part of the conditions of our modern world. What we are dealing with at this time is the same impulse that has been active throughout human history, yet is the scale of the damage much greater; so great it threatens the viability of Mother Earth. She is already greatly compromised, and if present trends continue, only disaster will result for all life forms including human beings.

The primordial human of modern civilization, the prototypical model representing its values, its direction, and its justification, is the one who conquers through persistence, strength of will and talent, nature herself. Who seizes Mother Earth by the throat and makes her yield her secrets for the good and the progress of humanity. This good, this progress is understood as enrichment, as the increasing possession of material wealth by the individual. In the generalized view, this progressive enrichment is meant to be for all individuals; included in that is the willingness to allow certain ones to amass great wealth. They are considered the trailblazers who create wealth and make it possible for all to share in it. These individuals assume mythic proportions by virtue of their outsized effect on the economics of modern society. They do not wield mighty swords or hurl thunderbolts but they might as well for all the destructive power they demonstrate.

Modern economic gain at this stage of human evolution cannot be separated from the continued development and application of technology; technology that is new, or new uses for already existing technology. Thus is much of what we call wealth created through a developmental process that requires the extraction of more and more resources from the earth to directly and indirectly support the material foundation of this new wealth. The whole process is like a runaway train whose momentum is steadily gaining speed and feeding off itself, leaving increasing destruction in its wake.

What if you gave without thought of reward or recompense? To realize you have everything is to give without forethought or motive; to give wholeheartedly to all for Love is giving itself. There is no true giving without Love, and no Love without giving. To give truly is to love, and to love is to give truly. All that is good and true in this life must be shared as Love must be shared.

The totality of Being does not depend on the specific nor does it consist of details. Oneness is the same everywhere, at all times, for it is not in time. All things rest in It, and It is in all things yet is completely unaffected by form and difference. Being cannot be captured by what is partial and separate. Thought is always limited, always of the part, it cannot touch that which is whole and unbroken. To touch this Being you must be alive, vulnerable, without defenses. To defend is to close off; That which is openness Itself can only be reached through openness, by going beyond all limits that enclose and define. Beyond all enclosures, all limits, all attempts to capture and hold, is the vastness of Spirit Itself. That and That alone is your real home.

The beauty of this Vastness is its innocence, its untouchability. It is non-substantial, intangible, yet as real as a mountain, as the ocean. It has the same impenetrable, unconquerable strength. In comparison to Spirit, a mountain is like the smallest of pebbles underfoot, the ocean a small puddle. The impenetrable strength of Beingness Itself cannot be perceived or explained. It can only be experienced directly, within oneself. It waits for you on the border between the manifest and the unmanifest.

The Light of Mind filled the room; everyone was in It, there was nothing outside of It. It was like a force, a power, that lifted you out of yourself; an energy that penetrated mind and body. Nothing could resist That for It was part of you, a part that you did not know perhaps. It came from beyond the border of everyday experience, beyond time and the things of time. Space and time cannot contain It or limit It in any way.

Through the application of logic and reasoned argument, it is impossible to prove the existence of God definitively to everyone's satisfaction; likewise is it impossible to prove the nonexistence of God as you cannot prove a negative. So we are left once again with the question of the existence of the Transcendent. The question can only be answered on the level of the individual's subjective experience although we can say this is not as narrow a basis for coming to a conclusion as it may first appear. More than one individual can simultaneously experience something of the Transcendent at a given place and time. Though the nature of the experience remains subjective on the level of the individual, other individuals who are in objective relationship with that mind, and who also have the same experience at the same time, are an indication of verification in an objective sense.

The beauty of the lake was a fact not to be argued with or denied but accepted. A simple yet large depression in the earth filled with water and surrounded on all sides by pine trees. The description is simple yet the beauty of it is more than the words or the parts that together make up the Whole. Beauty is always of the Whole. Water is so simple and humble yet always in motion, driven by the wind, reflecting light from its surface. Always changing, never still as in a rushing stream, it sings unceasingly as it joyfully flows past every obstruction and reaches the majestic river where it continues its great journey at a more dignified pace, finally merging with its source, the great blue ocean. Then it rises again as vapor to become a cloud, and driven by the wind, returns to bless the earth as the life-giving rain. Life is like that, a ceaseless flow of form to form, birth to death then birth again until it merges into the great ocean of Being, returning to the Source it never left.

Early this morning upon awakening, there was a power, a pressure in the head for no reason, indescribable. It had nothing to do with the body, with the brain, yet it was emptying out the brain leaving only silence. The mind itself was silent; this power came from beyond the mind, yet was centered in the mind and its instrument, the brain, like a purifying force. It was a fire burning away the past, all thought and feeling, all memory. It could not be described or captured by thinking; it was free beyond all imagining. It comes from beyond the known, beyond the net of thought which is always a stale repetition of past experience, conditioning, and future projections. It was the unknown, penetrating the known, pushing it aside, uncovering the depths of mind that wait beneath the surface of everydayness. The freedom that is inherent to mind, though seldom discovered, is covered up by the accretions of centuries of conditioning, of habit. The mind is made dull by the constant movement of fear and desire, forced into a narrow band of experience, missing the glory and beauty all around it both within and without. The action of this power frees the mind, dissolving the barriers that limit it. The unknown is free beyond thought or measure, beyond description or experience. You cannot experience it. The you must be absent for it to be.

There is a Presence that is everywhere; It is not separate

from anything and yet beyond everything. It cannot be grasped, held; It will always slip through your fingers if you try. Within you and all around you, the Presence waits for you to notice, to recognize and join with It. You need do nothing, just let It be and be present.

To do the right thing is often the hardest of all. The right thing is not done for personal gain, for selfish reasons. To do right is to do what is best for all no matter what the circumstances, to recognize that all interests are part of a common interest that must be addressed in any action. No one can be left out or ignored for all are part of the whole. The good of the whole is the proper concern of government at all levels. What appears as individual self-interest must at times be sacrificed in the interest of the whole. This is unavoidable and is balanced out by the good the individual receives as a part of the collective.

The good of the whole is seldom the concern of the private sector, of business in general, for business itself arises from individual self-interest and pursues individual goals whether they be of one owner or of many shareholders who together own a company. Even if many, however, they are pursuing their interest (to make a profit) on a narrow basis for personal gain. The good of the whole is not considered. That is simply the nature of all activities whose motive is individual gain exclusively. This cannot be denied or avoided entirely.

In our current era, this pursuit of profit for a relatively small group of individuals or one individual increasingly does not simply ignore the interests of the whole society but is, with increasing momentum, actually accomplished maximally for the benefit of the few to the detriment of the whole. There is nothing new about this except the scale of the damage it is beginning to inflict. Society as a whole is being increasingly impacted by this activity and weakened as a result. The mechanisms of government charged with regulating economic behavior to prevent damage to society are more and more ineffective at controlling and limiting damage due to political pressure and interference. The political pressure is a result of economic interests that exert undue and greater and greater control over the political process. Those who are pursuing their interests at the expense of the whole are more and more in the position of removing all reasonable restraints on their behavior, leaving them to pursue their own economic interests without regard for the greater society in which they live. That this is a situation that is inherently unstable and destructive to the well-being of society in general is rather obvious. Human behavior being as it is, and based greatly on individual self-interest, no system of government in which the self-interest of a minority is allowed to prevail at the expense of the majority can fail to become corrupt over time. Corruption degrades the ability of the government to secure the greater interest, the interest of the whole society, and the continuing and increasing inequality becomes established, along with a whole system of both governmental and private institutions whose function is to defend, justify, and maintain this status quo.

Just sitting right now, It came; an indescribable and indefinable Light that was Whole. You can be in It and of It, but you can never touch It with your mind, with thought. This light comes and goes as It will; desire cannot attract It nor can will hold It. Light is freedom Itself, a lightness and beauty forever beyond limitation, ungraspable, unknowable within the confines of identity. Mind and Light are one and the same; there is no separation between them. The Mind shines by its own intrinsic Light, a Light that illuminates the universe. You are that Light as is everything in existence without exception. All is Light, only Light; shadows appear within It and move about, the figures of the everyday world. Everything is the play of Light, nothing more, nothing less.

The purity that is life can never be touched by the ego mind. The mind identified as the ego, as separate and separative being, can only play at life, can manipulate and try to control the conditions and circumstances it faces, but never can it actually live in the purity and beauty that is life itself. The mind identified with a body, devoted to pursuing its own desires and goals, is dull and lifeless no matter its accomplishments. It can excel in its physicality, its mental activity, inventiveness; these are pale shadows of life itself, counterfeits as life's expressions, though there may be some value in all of that.

Life is a movement of the Whole. It comes from beyond the mind, the me. It is not the body that is alive. The body lives through the reflected light of Mind. Life is that Light and more as the river is more than the motion that propels it to the sea. You cannot define life or capture it in words, surround it with names, descriptions and concepts. The word, the name, is not alive. The products of the intellect are static, bound by the past, by habit and memory. They cannot keep up with what is always new, flowing, in a constant state of transformation. Its beauty is beyond the petty knowledge of the intellect, beyond thought and feeling.

The great forests are vanishing, victims of the greed that drives the huge, insatiable, forever hungry beast that is the modern economy. The great beast is devouring the very ground beneath its feet; in its greedy, restless madness, it does not seem to notice or perhaps it does not care. Like a very large animal with a very small head, it is aware of nothing but its hunger, the hunger of its billions of cells, the humans and their organizations that make up its vast body. No one cell is aware of the extent of the destruction for which it too bears responsibility. Thus is it easy to claim innocence by virtue of ignorance. The ignorance of many may lead to the death of all eventually. The result of our great war upon the earth is not in doubt, only the timing of its end is open to speculation.

Surely it is madness to wage war upon the very basis of your survival. We are committing planetary suicide and in our commitment to self-destruction, to sinking the ark on which we live, we are willing to take down with us all life with which we share existence. And yet, if I was to speak to this issue as boldly as these words imply, I would meet and have met with anger, defensiveness, and denial, even personal attack. It seems to be a very common human response to shoot the messenger who brings the bad news or at least throw stones at him and defame his character if possible.

There is a segment of our population who hold liberal progressive views and generally favor curbing or minimizing environmental destruction. Much legislation has been passed with that aim. Despite being well-meaning, none of these measures even begin to address the real problem that lies at the heart of our dilemma. Recycling, electric cars etc. while perhaps mildly helpful are at best like Band-Aids, plastered around a gaping wound that is pouring blood. They do not even begin to stop the flow much less do they remove the dagger that is plunged into the heart of Mother Earth. The obsession with greenhouse gases, with controlling our carbon output is almost like a diversionary tactic to keep humanity fighting over something that is relatively minor in comparison to the overall picture. It seems to me almost as if there is a sense in the minds of many that we are in great danger, but to face that danger honestly would require a radical change in consciousness and how we live, and this very few are willing to do. So the urge to do something focuses on a peripheral issue that will not address the cause but at least leaves us with the impression that we are doing something helpful, like a kind of pressure valve that releases enough pressure to produce some relief but does not change the force building up or reduce its destructive capacity.

The night is still, waiting. An expectant hush has fallen over the forest. There is a quality of expectation; the trees know something is coming. They wait, endlessly patient, as they have waited so many times before. Never are they disappointed, they do not know disappointment or discouragement. The essence of a tree is patience. To grow it depends on sun and rain, the quality of the soil that holds its roots, and the goodwill of other trees around it. They grow together the trees of the forest. Together they suffer drought, fire, snow and rain, the scorching sun in summer. Never do they complain; even when being cut down they suffer their fate silently. Their shade is given impartially to all, the seeds or nuts they produce likewise. The forest loves silently, gives silently, lives each day never knowing what tomorrow may bring.

The concern about tomorrow, the uncertainty of things to come, casts a shadow across the mind. It's hard for human beings to live with this uncertainty, this not knowing what to expect. To expect is to be able to plan, to erect defenses against contingencies. The mind is always planning, always in control if possible. The present is rigidly organized, arranged to meet the perceived needs of the day, and to avoid discomfort or unpleasantness. Tomorrow must be a continuation of today with its habits, its pleasures, its little comforts. You may succeed for a day, a week, a year, even longer, but always life is waiting to enter your little fantasy of happiness and control.

Events that move the world and intrude upon the life of the individual have their own causes and reasons, their own rhythm. They do not conform themselves to our needs and wishes. And death, the great leveler of all playing fields, has its own appointed time to visit and bring an end to all vain imaginings and restless strivings.

The present era we are about to enter (or have already entered) will be one of great change, even traumatic change. All our institutions will be greatly challenged. Our cherished way of life based on overconsumption, overstimulation, and the selfish pursuit of whatever catches our fancy will become impossible to maintain. It was never a way of life that could be viable in the long run. A life based on such conspicuous wastage of the earth's bounty, the overconsumption of energy resources, and the production of so many artificial materials and poisonous byproducts, could never be anything less than an environmental disaster. It is a sad fact of human history that societies do not change or correct their self-destructive ways voluntarily but rather are forced to change by external factors over which they have no control.

Our civilization seems to be no exception to this rule despite the commonly held belief that our science and technology have nature and life well under control. The appearance of control is but another modern illusion. Nature is indeed suffering under our domination but she is by no means under control. In fact, the more we try to control her, to dominate her according to our will, the more damage we do. And, as we are dependent on the cooperation of nature, as our very lives depend upon it, to wreak havoc with the natural world will only come back to haunt us. We are dependent upon the soil, the rains, and natural sources of water to sustain human life. And we cannot forget the weather, its patterns of hot and cold, of rainfall and storms, all of which impact our lives in different ways. The present pattern of global warming, for example, is affecting food supplies and water supplies in certain areas, putting much stress on the population there and the local economies.

What is forgotten by modern civilization, in its love affair with power, control and domination, is the inconvenient fact that for all our technological prowess and the abstraction of our way of life bordering on alienation, we are nevertheless undeniably embedded in a much larger system: the planet as a whole and all life upon it. An attitude towards the whole that gives it value only in proportion to the resources we can extract from it for economic gain is both shortsighted and seriously flawed. Shortsighted in that economic considerations are notoriously obsessed with immediate gain at the expense of long-term sustainability, and flawed in the sense of being willing to destroy or seriously damage the balance and viability of whole areas of life or natural systems on which our lives may or do depend. The pollution of the oceans which provide, or did provide, much food for humanity in the past is one such example; the polluting or destruction of the water table in certain areas from which the local population draws its drinking water is another. To destroy whole systems on which life depends to obtain short-term gain is surely beyond shortsighted. It is destructively selfish and completely insane.

Human nature is, alas, only too capable of and prone to deny the self-destructiveness of its activities for the sake of economic gain. We are too willing to shoot ourselves in the foot individually and collectively if we can deny that we are so doing and the limp that results is not too noticeable. Unfortunately, at this present moment in our history, we are not just using our feet for target practice but are blasting away at our internal organs also. When the bleeding will stop is anyone's guess but I think it will be sooner rather than later.

Through the pale covering of cloud, the moon gleams, misty and indistinct. Her pale radiance illuminates the darkness. Without a flashlight, I walk along through the cool, damp night. Always I feel the forest is waiting for some mysterious, unknown communication. The night herself is listening, silent and still. Only the sound of my footsteps, the gravel crunching beneath my feet, and far off the harsh croaking of a tree frog calling for a mate.

Go out tonight and sit silently on the earth, where the noises of civilization cannot be heard. Leave the day behind, its cares and activities forgotten, and give yourself to the night. Let its soft, enveloping darkness soothe your heart and mind. Let the mind be still for a moment and feel... Something is waiting for you, waiting for you to notice; deep within yet all around you. You are part of It and part of everything that shares its life with you. This has been forgotten, a dim memory from a bygone time, yet without this, you are not fully a human being, but a mechanical creature lost in the madness of a society where life has been turned into a race without a finish line. Ask yourself this question: Is this what I want, is this how I want to live? Do I like what my life has become? Do I like what I am becoming? The answers may not be forthcoming, it does not matter. What matters is to start the inquiry, to question. Try to take an honest look at your life, its activities, your feelings and moods. Where is it going? Look at where it has been and you will know where it's going. More of the same if that is what you want. Is it? Is that what you want?

The day is cool and sunny, the air crisp, the wind silent, waiting for the next storm to give it strength again. The forest is happy, rejoicing in the recent rain, grateful for this reprieve from the drought. The forest floor, covered with a mat of pine needles and oak leaves, is still damp and the leaves are starting to decay, returning their life and nutrients to the soil. Not so long ago, only the original inhabitants of this forest, of these hills and mountains, moved carefully and respectfully along the old trails, establishing their encampments where there was water and level ground. Life was not so comfortable then, hardship more a part of everyday experience. An attunement to the earth, to her changing cycles and moods, and a simplicity and reverence for life characterized the consciousness of the people.

Something has been lost since then. An alien civilization entered the forested hills seeking the yellow metal known as gold. The invaders went crazy over it, stopping at nothing to find it and extract it from the earth. They cut down the trees and dug up the streams. Anyone or anything that got in their way was killed or driven out.

Nowadays, in the small town built by the miners, there is a humble monument to the people who were here before; a small teepee-shaped structure built of slabs of wood, the original type of dwelling that once housed the men and women who walked these forests, fished in her streams and rivers, worshipped the Creator in their own way and thanked their Earth Mother for her bounty. Perhaps this simple structure is a fitting tribute to their way of life; a stark contrast to the society that followed. Around this simple structure the streets are busy with traffic; many steel boxes on wheels, each ferrying one or more persons from who knows where to who knows where or why. Behind it is the freeway and yet more restless movement, a constant coming and going, a blur of speed and purpose. The more modern buildings that surround the simple structure dwarf it by their size but lack the dignity, the simplicity and humility that are effortlessly part of it.

There is a plaque fastened to a post beside it that states this structure is a proud tribute to honor the original people who inhabited these hills. It does not say that we killed them or drove them out and took their land. Evidently, we weren't proud of them then. Now that we have everything and they are left with almost nothing, we are proud. Better late than never I guess.

The forests, the hills and mountains and streams and rivers are waiting for their return. You can feel the presence of the ones who lived here before us, not only here but all across America. The deserts and canyons, the high plains, the snow-covered mountains and deep forests; all are waiting for the vanished ones to return. Everywhere I feel it, unseen but still there; their spirits surround us watching, waiting for their time to come again. The forest in which I presently live patiently waits for us to go and leave it in peace. It bears us no grudge for the damage we have done, for our ingratitude for what it has given us, for the careless and unthinking pain we have inflicted upon the earth.

The earth has seen many empires and civilizations come and go, each marked by human arrogance and pride, and driven by greed and the lust for power. Each has erected its great monuments to its gods, its rulers. All now sleep, covered by the dust of history. Only scattered ruins and the bones of many buried deep in the earth remain; their spirits gone on to we know not where. Soon we too will share their fate. Our civilization has been perhaps the most arrogant of all. Great technological developments and scientific knowledge have given us a control over nature greater than ever before. And we have done unprecedented damage on a large scale to the living and natural systems of the earth. Unlike the ones that preceded us who recognized their dependence on nature and her cycles to some degree at least, we seem to deny any such reciprocity. The curious belief that we stand above and beyond nature without any responsibility towards her will be our downfall. That and the greedy restlessness that characterizes the modern Western mind and drives its economy of infinite growth and unrestrained development.

In each one of us there is a spark of Light, the great creative Light of the universe. It lies hidden in most, covered over by ignorance, delusory thinking, and the accretions of centuries. Modern life, its priorities and values, seems almost designed to maintain ignorance of the spiritual reality within and intent on perpetuating it. The consensus reality of the theory of materialism denies, obstructs and, in the minds of many, "disproves" the existence of anything but the material universe. That this is fundamentally delusion and wishful thinking based simply on the conditioning influence of the media, secular education, and limited experience goes unrecognized. The belief system that is materialism is believed by its adherents to be reality itself; the map of reality, that is all any belief system really is, is confused with the territory it supposedly describes, Reality as it exists in and of itself beyond concepts and beliefs. Clearly and obviously, a map is not the territory it attempts to represent. The map of California is not the reality or actuality that is the state of California. This fact is very apparent and easy to grasp. To see clearly one's belief system or all belief systems as but maps and thus perceive their true relationship to what they symbolize is more difficult to comprehend and thus prone to much confusion.

The mind invents belief systems and believes in and identifies with what it has made. To identify is to make it part of yourself, and you will assert and defend what is part of you and be very reluctant to let it go. That this process is, for the most part, automatic and unconscious makes it very difficult for the human mind to understand its thinking, not the thoughts themselves but the whole process of what we think and why.

The consensus view of reality that dominates our modern civilization, academia, science and scholarship, is simply a mental construct and is a very limited and partial view of reality. The limitations placed on free thinking and true understanding today by the maintenance and defense of consensus reality are every bit as stifling and obstructive to real understanding as those of earlier times such as the medieval period. Although today's pressure towards conformity of thought is generally more subtle, it is nonetheless just as pernicious and constant, especially in some areas of human endeavor.

No one can argue with a fact. The sunrise is a fact and does not elicit argument. It is in the interpretation of facts where disagreements and arguments come in. A belief about something in the sense of right or wrong, good or bad, true or delusory, always rests on interpretation of the fact or facts in question. We might react emotionally to a fact but this does not affect it. I may not like that the sun rises in the east and sets in the west, preferring some other arrangement, yet the sun continues merrily on its way, on its appointed rounds, completely unconcerned. I am unlikely to get into conflict with another over the fact that is the sunrise. The interpretation of that fact or of my response to it is where the possibility of conflict arises.

To attempt to uncover the great mystery hidden within requires real interest, passion, and dissatisfaction with the apparent limits placed on your life by the intellect and previous experience. To the obstructions, distractions, and noise that continually draw your attention outward is added the innate resistance of the egoic identity to truth. All this must be understood and overcome. The Truth that you are is not some objectively perceptible fact or set of facts that can be reduced to perception. Reality is what you are beyond body and mind as you know it; that is your real identity. As such, Reality must be directly experienced from within as part of you; just as you, to some degree at least, experience your present surface identity, your humanness as you.

A different kind of experience is required on what is commonly described as the spiritual path or the path to Truth. The spiritual, what is most fundamental as existence, is its own dimension of Being; Being that is transcendent and yet right here, right now. What is required is a reorientation of the mind, a realignment that will permit the direct experience of what is most real. Perception must be purified and corrected that it be whole rather than partial. All false ideas and beliefs, indeed in most cases the entire belief system,. must be undone, given up, recognized as false and fundamentally useless.

Sometimes the silence is so loud you can actually hear it. Some mystics say that silence is the Voice of God. Others say that you can only hear God speak in silence. In any case, the constant busyness of mind must be stilled, must come to a stop if you are to hear the Voice of God. Your own soul or spirit speaks to you through silence. In deep stillness of mind and heart, what you truly want and need will be revealed to you if that is your wish.

Now that the rain has stopped, a hush has fallen over the forest. The trees stand silent, the only movement the water dripping from the leaves. The wind is finished for the day; it will be back tomorrow or maybe tonight, bringing more rain. The forest has been drinking it in for days yet is eager for more. The forest must drink its fill now for with the spring comes warm weather and the rains will stop then.

Silence is an amazing thing. Not the silence that is the absence of sound but the Silence in which all things arise. This Silence can be heard when the mind is very quiet, when the superficial surface activity has ceased and the sense of attention rests in the depths of mind. Silence is unceasing; It is the background against which all things occur. Unaffected by the noise and activity of life, It remains pure and empty. You cannot manufacture this Silence; It will not be found through effort or struggle. It must come to you unbidden, on Its own terms, a great mystery that is untouchable. Yet you are always in It whether aware of It or not.

Today the rain has stopped, the low hanging clouds that blanketed the hills have lifted. The clouds that remain float high above the land. They are almost white with shadings of gray, not the heavy dark gray of yesterday. Very slowly they move, in no hurry to go anywhere unlike the rain clouds driven by the wind who seem to want always to move on, to bring their precious gift of rain to the high mountain ridges in the distance and the desert that lies just beyond. Occasionally there is a break in the cloud cover and the sun shines through briefly. You can feel the promise of spring for a moment, the light is brighter, carrying a hint of the warmth that is to come. In the middle of each season, the season that follows is born. Here in the depths of winter, spring is patiently waiting like the trees of the forest. They are enjoying the rain yet they look forward to the return of the sun and its warmth that they may begin to grow again and clothe themselves in new foliage.

What is the price of success? What does it cost you, what must you give up, what sacrifices must be made? The rewards of success: Money, power, recognition and fame, do they justify, compensate for what is lost? Success is the result of competition with your fellows. Competition is an ugly, heartless thing. Ruthless striving, trampling over one another, always some left by the wayside, for with competition there must inevitably be winners and losers. Always there is great wastage of energy and loss of goodwill. Humanly, much is lost through the excesses and selfishness of competition; both the individual and society bear the cost of the controlled warfare that is competition. Mother Earth herself suffers much of the damage from our economic competition. Success is not necessarily efficient in its use of resources that must be extracted from Mother Earth and her natural systems. A relative efficiency on the part of one company within the framework of its competitive success over others does not reduce the overall wastage and overconsumption of resources that result from an overcompetitive economy. One may triumph for a while but all will eventually lose.

There is something in which we live, move, and have our Being. Our lives arise within This and take place in It. In everything we do, we express It and represent It or we act out our ignorance and separation from It. To be separate from the ground of our Being is to be separate from everyone and everything we see; yet they too are part of Being as is all true existence. In Buddhism, one of the "poisons," as they are called, that separates us from what we are in Truth, is ignorance of our true nature. This ignorance along with other factors leads to errors of understanding and motivation that reinforce and extend the original error of separation from our Creative Source.

It is impossible to feel and believe yourself separate from all around you and not feel afraid. This fundamental fear is controlled, suppressed, and denied, but all fears that plague human life and drive our behavior arise from this one original mistake, this fundamental error. What can be done? All the wisdom traditions, the spiritual traditions of humanity, offer a response and a solution to this one error of thought, belief, and experience. The solution is, most simply, a return to the truth of your Being, a state of Oneness that is transcendent and yet includes all that you see and experience.

The day was bright and sunny, not a cloud to mar the perfection of the deep blue sky. The winter light was bright but not harsh like the light of summer that overwhelms the eyes and bleaches out the bright colors of spring. The crisp air was pleasant to breathe, yet without the chill that causes you to button up your coat. A day of great beauty and promise, welcoming yet not overly friendly although the rain and snow were finished for now. You could relax for awhile, sit in the mild sunshine and admire the beauty of the surrounding hills.

Beauty is said to be in the eyes of the beholder; it rises rather in the mind, in the capacity of the mind to recognize something ineffable yet there, impossible to describe in essence but directly experienced through the heart and mind. Beauty is the quality of life, of experience, that echoes and reflects the perfection that is Truth Itself. The immense beauty and delight of our true condition is faintly present in the beauty of the natural world. The creativity of the human mind expressed through the Arts is the attempt, however veiled, to represent the primal beauty and order from which we come.

If you sit quietly, listening and feeling, the chattering mind still and empty, Life Itself will begin to communicate with you. The trees and hills and rocks will share their feelings. These are not the emotions of human life, self-justifying, self-important; just the simple quality of being itself, the delight of existence. If you really listen, you can hear the One Voice behind them all. That Voice will speak to you if you make room for It, a quiet place within the mind where the ego is absent, where you listen with real humility and receptivity.

The human mind often overestimates its understanding. We think we know things that are unknowable but through experience, experience that we have not had. Each of us tries to find the answer to life, its problems and uncertainties, in his/ her own way. As long as our answer seems to work, we look no further. We have our ducks all in a row and that is good enough until something happens to upset our comfortable little scenario. Again we seek a specific solution, one that will restore the conditions required, one that will last. The great obsession of the modern world is to have a life of comfort, security, sameness, pleasure and satisfaction; a life in which I can maintain the avoidance of suffering and the denial of death. Suffering will come, it waits its turn patiently. Maybe tomorrow, next week, next month, or next year, but it will visit us no matter what we do, no matter how grand our life and our opinion of our self. Life cannot be controlled; to believe so is to live out illusions thinking them true. Illusions will always fail you. To believe otherwise is madness.

The great illusion of modern life: that happiness and security can be found through control of material circumstances. While it is true that a kind of seeming happiness, a superficial sort of feeling content may be found when circumstances are favorable, i.e. material needs are met, family life and work are satisfactory, even fulfilling, and there is sufficient stimulation, distraction and entertainment to keep the mind busy. This happiness depends on the maintenance of certain conditions of life and life itself is always changing, sometimes for the better, sometimes for the worse. The mind itself is subject to varying moods and feelings that are the result of the conditioning of the past and the response to the ongoing events of daily life. In the midst of a life of changing conditions, physical, mental, emotional, circumstantial, no matter how stable life seems to be in its core – home, health, family, work etc., nothing is guaranteed to last. The body continues to age, the children grow up, friends seem to come and go, and each has their own set of problems. Economic changes, political upheavals, social tensions and conflict, the constant introduction of new technology, and always the constant drumbeat, an unbroken barrage of pressure to buy this, buy that, do this, go here; the incessant drone of advertising aimed at persuading you to buy what you do not need never stops.

Can happiness or peace be found on the level of the bodily

identity? Is it even possible in the midst of the chaos, frantic activity, and change that is modern life? To seek for happiness where it cannot be found is surely not the way to find it. A counterfeit happiness, changing, ephemeral, here one day and gone the next, will never satisfy you or bring the peace you desire and need. Only disappointment, with hopes raised high then dashed again and again, futility marking your life at every turn, will be the result of putting your trust where it is not warranted.

How do we know what we know? Who knows it? What is knowing actually? What is it to know something? What does knowing entail? Do I know unless I know that I know (Self Awareness)? To know something is to be aware of it, i.e. to say I know it's raining outside means I am aware of the rain falling – I see it or hear it. So outer perception is part of this everyday knowing. I also know I have thoughts and feelings, how? I know through a kind of inner hearing or feeling, again perception is involved. Can I know something directly without the medium of perception? For example, the most basic thing I know is that I exist, I am. Even with eyes closed and in a state of mind where I do not feel the body such as in a state of paralysis; if I am aware, then I know I exist just by the fact that I am aware. I would not question that fact. So what then is the basis for knowing? Awareness of Self or Self Awareness with or without perception seems to be the basis of knowing; hence knowing is a direct property or characteristic of awareness itself. Perception is then a secondary characteristic of awareness as it cannot occur unless there is knowing of its occurrence.

Without knowledge of the Self
Mind is able to hear
And see only its own projections.
Not knowing from where it comes
Or where it goes.

Mind knows
By virtue of a reflected light
That is not its own.
Incessant activity of thought
Covers the Light by which it sees.

Deep beneath the surface
Beyond restless waves of thought
Ocean like stillness
The peace of the ages
Light shines brightly.

What is it to know something? What is this thing you know? Do you actually "know it" or do you simply have an idea about it which you take for knowledge, or you perceive it and note its form, size, location, and maybe certain other characteristics and you likewise take these perceptions for knowledge?

Perception is an unreliable and often changing process. A number of people may observe an interaction between two persons, an event where something transpired. Questioned separately, no two witnesses will have the same story as to what they saw though all perceived the same happening at the same time. Perception is affected by the feelings, moods, states of mind, values etc. of the perceiver. Perception always involves a kind of sorting out, a conscious or unconscious decision on what elements to focus on, what to ignore and so on. Perception always involves interpretation of what is perceived. With all these variables and the changes they may go through, can we say that perception is a reliable guide to knowing?

Much of our human knowing is simply belief about something. Belief is based on opinions, values, whatever degree of personal experience we may have had, memory; in other words there is a host of factors that affect and condition our minds leading to the beliefs we hold. These factors may vary greatly from person to person. Any given thing may be regarded in many different and even contradictory ways. Yet each will believe his/her belief is right, i.e. that he/she knows what is true. Much of what passes for knowing is nothing of the kind. Perhaps it would be helpful for all of us to remember how much of what we think we know is simply belief based on opinion, on our individual biases.

Either you will listen to the voice of reason or you won't. Reason will guide you in the ways of love and kindness. It will bring you together with your brothers, not keep you apart, isolated and estranged. Reason will lead you back to the Self you never left though you have forgotten It and blocked Its memory from your awareness. The exercise of reason will set your feet on the path that leads back to God, to the Source of all that lives. To listen to reason is to return to true sanity and forsake the madness that grips the human mind, filling it with fear and trembling. All hatred and attack arise from the fear that pervades the mind at all levels. Heal this fear, release it from all its hiding places, uncover it under all its disguises and renounce it wherever it is operating, and only love will remain and you will know freedom again.

Reason does not argue. It has no need for conflict or disputation. Fear breeds conflict, giving rise to attack and defense. Where conflict rules, sanity and reason are absent. Conflict feeds on fear and hatred; a recurring cycle is thus set in motion perpetuating itself thereby and reinforcing the fear that drives it. Whatever thinking does not follow reason is of the ego, the separating and separative identity that lives only for itself. To live only for yourself will isolate you from the flow of life. Life itself is inclusive, denying no one and embracing all. There are no separate "bits" of life, living apart from the Whole, threatening and threatened by other equally separate "bits," a seething mass of separate beings fighting with one another and everything around them, struggling to impose order on chaos. Certain it is that judging by appearances this is the case;

appearances, however, are always misleading and partial, and Reality Itself transcends appearance and the reactions to it. If you lead a life based merely on the appearance of things, you will be caught in a never-ending cycle of reaction, both within and without, to the false impressions created by a mind that believes it is what it is not.

Mind is like a wheel attached to a stationary axle. It goes round and round and round, seeming to go somewhere when in actuality it goes nowhere as it endlessly repeats itself while staying in the same place. The stream of feeling and thought, impulses and images, is constantly busy; yet it is the busyness of repetition, of wearying habit and routine, much noise and chaotic activity signifying exactly nothing.

The desert is like an almost empty easel, waiting for life to populate it with images. The sky above is vast, seemingly stretching forever, its continuation broken only by distant mountain ranges. There is a kind of beauty in the monotone coloration so characteristic of desert landscapes, the endless light brown of the earth, the bright bursts of yellow flowers on the rabbit bush, the gray green of the sagebrush, the irregular green shapes of the cacti. Above the endless blue and the fleecy white clouds that flow slowly, placidly, across the vastness of the sky. And always the sun, brightly shining as it moves slowly through the day, baking everything below under its relentless gaze.

The great ship sails on through the night
Ignoring icebergs all around,
Dead ahead the largest one of all.
The ship of state is unsinkable.
Delusions will not die,
They just change form
And reappear in new clothing
To suit the age.

The mighty ship did sink
Yet it sails again across the seas
Heedless as before,
Larger, more advanced, unconscious.

Constantly rearranging the deck chairs
Passengers keep themselves busy.
The crew goes about their tasks,
Never looking up, they see no danger.
Surprises are not surprises for
Those who are prepared.

What is preparation?
To see without shrinking from what is seen.
To think without motive, leaving
All wishful fantasies behind.
Be willing to help others who cannot see.
Blindness is contagious, it spreads among those
Who would not open their eyes.
The blind cannot lead, they must follow
Those who see with their mind
And know with their heart.

Since mind as such, pure from the beginning, having no root to hold to,
something other than itself, having nothing to do with an agent
or something to be done, one may well be happy.
Longchenpa

Chapter 3

To Find Peace

There is a way to find peace, even in a world that denies and attacks it. Beneath the surface of things as they appear to be is the state of peace and happiness that is Reality Itself. Everything you see around you, the earth, the sky, the trees, the streets and buildings, is but the thinnest of skins like the skin of a balloon. This thinnest of skins is stretched over and conceals something vast and unimaginable, a Light and Being that is infinite, and That, That alone is real.

Surely it seems like insanity to be told what you see before you is a dream, filled with illusory figures that come and go, flickering shadows, nothing more. That is not your experience at all. Your life and everything in it seems real, substantial, and has real effects. Objects seem solid, dense; they occupy space and are clearly separated from you by the intervening space.

Are objects really solid? Science has discovered that 99% of the apparent volume occupied by a physical object is actually empty space. That includes the earth on which you stand and your own body. The solidity and fixed quality of the world you see is only a seeming, a seeming determined in its appearance by your perception. You probably think that pretty much everyone sees the same world you do, sees it in the same way. However, experiments done by psychologists as well as the experience of law enforcement authorities in interviewing multiple witnesses to a crime indicate clearly the variable nature of individual perception, even of the same event.

Perception always involves interpretation and the sorting out of perceptual data. This process is influenced by the state of mind of the perceiver, the values they hold, past conditioning and experience, and even by their emotional state. To trust your perception to reveal Reality to you is simply an error, albeit a very common one. Human perception is always flawed, always partial. It perceives neither the whole nor its parts accurately. To grasp, to understand and eventually experience the Real directly, you must go beyond human perception which shows you only the surface of things, never their Reality.

The evening is still, motionless, quite cold, with a dampness that penetrates. The cloudless sky is bright with stars glittering everywhere. The tall trees stand waiting, dark against the sky, motionless, waiting as they have always done. There is a faint but steady sound in the distance, perhaps a few crickets who have survived the winter so far, awakened from their winter sleep by the warmth and sunshine of the past few days. Their song is muted, slower, not the happy song of summer that fills the night until dawn nor the sad yet loud chorus of autumn as their numbers steadily dwindle. Their autumn song is softer than in summer, a farewell to their fellows who have gone, a lament for the happy days gone by, melancholy yet beautiful. Some will survive the winter to begin again the growth of their numbers in the spring and the chorus will start, slowly at first then steadily louder till the warm evenings of summer are filled with their triumphant song.

Everything has its place, its way of being. All of nature is an expression of the one intelligence behind all existence. Life and all its forms is beautiful, mysterious, contradictory, puzzling, violent yet tender. From where does it come and where does it go? This the question each must answer. No one can answer for you. You can be helped, can be shown the answer in one form or another; yet you must find your own way with it, make the answer a part of you. No thinking, mere mentation, or emotional response is adequate to reach that depth where all fear is laid to rest, where the Sacred waits for your return.

What to do about the violence, the brutality of life? Violence begets more violence, never is there an end to it. The violence "out there" is not separate from you. It is a part of every mind. In a very real sense, it's not somebody else in the Middle East or elsewhere that is torturing and killing, it's me, it's you; the human mind is one. Within every mind lies the seeds of anger, hatred, the potential for violence; our anger and rage towards one another and the conflict and attack it engenders in our everyday life is not essentially different from the conflict and violence of war. It differs only in degree.

Superficially it appears as if belief and difference motivate the division, prejudice, and violence that have always marked human life. The belief in different gods, different religions, different social and political systems, seems to be the impetus behind the wars and atrocities of our day. In other cases, tribal divisions, ethnic and racial divisions seem to be the cause. Are these truly the causes or are they simply the reasons that justify hatred and violence? The actual cause is deeper, beneath the conceptual level of thought and belief. There is fear and a potential for violence waiting in the depths of every human mind.

Alexander Solzhenitsyn was a famous Russian writer who had spent many years in the Stalin-era Gulag of labor camps in Siberia. Once he was asked by a journalist if he regretted all the time he had lost in that long and brutal imprisonment. He did not regret those lost years, he told the journalist, because he had learned something very important. He had learned that the line separating good and evil does not pass through nations nor between social classes nor between political parties; the line separating good and evil runs right through the center of every human heart, through all human hearts.

The fear, envy, judgment, anger, and selfishness that operate in our human life are responsible for the conflict that arises in big and little ways. Individual conflict when magnified to the level of a social or ethnic group or nation becomes war or some other form of mass violence. We are not separate from the need to make war on our brothers though we may not be the ones pulling the trigger.

There is deep within each of us a memory of our origin. Lost to most by constant absorption in the life of the body, its ceaseless activity and the consistent busyness of the mind, the memory nonetheless remains, unaffected by the turmoil taking place on the surface of consciousness. This memory contains the experience of what was before time and will be again. It will wait until you are ready and willing to dive beneath the surface and penetrate the depths of mind.

The day began clear and cool, the clouds to the east reflecting the rising sun glowed a bright orange yellow. The color was intense against the pale blue sky and the day was bright and alive with the promise the new always brings. The new is not some unexpected version of what has always been, the past dressed in different clothing. It can never be expected or anticipated or it is not the new. There is no continuation of the past into the present except in the superficial sense of day to day tasks and responsibilities. Even these, however, are not the same as yesterday's. Time flows on, a river that is unstoppable, leaving nothing untouched, nothing as it was before. The mind imposes a dull, seeming continuity on its experience, a continuity that is not there. Even the mind itself is constantly changing; not the same today as it was yesterday. The memory of past habit and experience casts a shadow across the present. While you see today through yesterday's eyes, you will not see what is really there rising to greet you. The new has never been before; it is fresh, alive. Love is like that, always rediscovering itself, never stale or repetitious. The mind must free itself from the fetters of what has gone before and from the imaginations of the future. Living in the past, constantly worrying about the future, makes the mind dull, imprisoned by habit, routine and fear. You can never discover the new unless your mind is fresh, alive to the present. That which is beyond time cannot be found in the past, in memory or imagination. You must meet It in the present with all your attention, with new eyes and a mind that is open, receptive, unencumbered by experience and expectation. Then the new can be born within you; in that is creation, life, love and the death of the old. The old cannot be long maintained in the light of the new. The denial of the new is the continuation of the old with its suffering and dull mediocrity.

A gentle hail was falling. The small hailstones covered the ground like three-dimensional snowflakes. They seemed to hop around like tiny living things, still feeling the freedom of the sky though they had fallen to earth. Soon they began to melt and before long were no more. Experience is like that, seemingly free at times then becoming static, fixed, as it gives way to the pull of gravity, returning to the conformity of the everyday. Yet life takes place under a sky that is ceaselessly changing, never the same, free as space itself. Space is free because it is formless, without boundaries. Mind in its essence is like that, not the constant chatter of thought, but the background in which thought appears, consciousness itself. Like the sky, consciousness is spacious and accommodating, unaffected by what moves across it.

The dark night was very cold, the sky glittering with the light of a thousand stars. Beneath the heavy silence you could feel the stillness of all of nature, as if she was holding her breath, waiting for something to happen. Often when I walk in these forests, I feel the forest waiting, waiting for us to go and leave it in peace. We, with our activities, have changed it so much it does not seem to be itself anymore. The big trees are all gone, cut down long ago to build homes and shops. Slowly they are coming back in places but it takes time, much time.

Mother Earth gives of herself gladly without asking anything in return. We take without gratitude, without appreciation; greedily we tear our resources from her body, destroying everything in our way leaving great heaps of debris, gouging deep holes. Our refuse clogs her streams, toxic chemicals poison her waters. The great forests have for the most part been cut down to make way for civilization or to provide resources for its needs. The great trees that once shaded the ground from the sun are long gone except for small groups of survivors, saved somehow from the chainsaws to become living museums, sad reminders of the grandeur that once was.

Can the mind approach each day as if it were the first day? Can you see the day, experience the day, look at everything around you with eyes that are innocent, seeing the uniqueness that is each moment? The mind burdened by the past, caught in the deep grooves of habit, security, and repetition, is dull and lifeless. You can live the same day over and over, or each day can be fresh, new and unique.

Life calls to you constantly asking, who are you? Why are you here? Where are you going? Do you answer those questions by the way you live, by how you treat those who share life with you? Or do you simply act out the same habit patterns, charging along, seeing the images of the past rather than the reality of each new day. To live out a life of habit and repetition makes the mind insensitive to the life around it. To live in the past, from the past, covering over the present with memory and past conditioning, is not to live at all. Rather it is a kind of living death. The walking dead are everywhere, always hurrying, seldom seeing the beauty and livingness that surrounds them. To live from the past, always hurrying towards the future, is to miss life itself which only takes place here and now.

What is economic life really? Is it the graphs and statistics that economists use to make their predictions and describe economic activity on a large scale? Is it the mass movement of goods and services throughout a national economy or across international borders? There are many ways to approach this subject. From the standpoint of the individual, is economics not material well-being: The meeting of the basic needs of life; food, clothing, shelter and the job or business that provides the income to meet these needs? Ultimately everything comes down to the life of individuals. Any collective, no matter how large, is made up of many individuals, and the success of the collective body rests on the satisfaction of the needs of its individual members. Life always takes place on the individual level. Economic life then should and is presumed to have as its goal the well-being of the individual. On a national level this means the well-being of as large a number of the individuals that make up a nation as possible; minimally at least a majority.

A rational observer cannot help but wonder at the excessive greed and lack of honest thinking that characterize our current economic situation. While it is true that greed has always been a major motivating force in economic life, the greed factor appears to be growing exponentially at this time. It seems like the more wealth certain people have, very often the more they want; so we have the spectacle of very wealthy individuals or investor groups of wealthy individuals willing to do almost anything to become even wealthier. Even trampling on the economic well-being of the many who are below them on the financial food chain. Greed is recognized in economic theory and seemingly receives high approval from the conservative side of the political spectrum and from conservative economists who seem to make up the greater part of the profession currently.

Greed, as an emotion, is inherently irrational and concerned only with individual interests, often at the expense of the whole. Theoretically, greed is somewhat restrained by the power of the government, at least in modern life, but with the increasing influence of big money in politics, the government as a countervailing force cannot be relied upon.

The hegemony of greed, both as a social value and a powerful force driving economics, does not support or engender a balanced or harmonious society. Greed is, by definition, a divisive and separative influence on human life and this at a time when our society as a whole is becoming more and more fragmented into different interest groups, each with their own agenda. It seems to me that presently even much of science is functioning at the behest of the profit motive regardless of whether its discoveries are beneficial for human beings or Mother Earth. Whatever we do, and this includes the men and women of science, as human beings we are very good at rationalizing and justifying our behavior and this holds doubly true for activities that benefit us economically. The result can be and often is disastrous in the greater sense.

The idea of progress is currently defined almost entirely in terms of technological advances and the increase of material well-being (i.e. more and more possessions, more and more gadgets and widgets). Yet surely the goal of progress should be to increase the common good and the well-being of the individual in a more complete sense. Technology does not inherently fulfill that goal. Some advances (I would actually call them retreats) in modern weaponry have clearly the opposite effect. Much of the current fixation with digital technology seems focused on inventing certain devices simply because we can, not because we need them or because they improve human life. There is no inherent gain from simply making life faster and easier. Up to a point that seems to be true, but currently we are subject to the law of diminishing returns in this regard. Do more and more apps to make more of life's tasks quicker and easier always increase the quality of life? Indeed, it looks to me as if much of humanity is simply marching in lockstep to whatever tunes the latest technological advances are playing.

Human life is beginning to resemble more and more an extended, never-ending childhood with most eyes fixed on the latest "toys" without considering whether they are needed or even truly helpful. The attention span of humanity appears to be getting shorter and shorter. You do not have to be a genius to realize this does not bode well for our future. Call me old-fashioned if you will, but I question whether human beings were meant to be reduced to passive consumers spending their time at shopping malls or sitting in easy chairs hypnotized by the latest technological fad, lost in the endless quest for artificial stimulation.

You can feel spring in the air though it is still mid-winter. The light is getting brighter, the sun higher in the sky. The day was pleasantly warm and sunny, just a few wispy clouds to counter the deep blue of the sky. Some of the tall pine trees looked quite ill with many dead needles, sometimes entire branches of them. The forest has suffered greatly during the drought; some trees are dead already, many others appear to be dying. Yet the forest itself will survive. These ancient hills have seen countless generations of trees come and go, many droughts and wet seasons. Deep snow or torrential rain, it is all the same to them. Everything has its season to flourish, its time to decay. All of life waxes and wanes with the seasons and with the cycle of years. Nothing stays the same for long; all things come and go in a ceaseless parade of passing images like moving shadows cast upon a wall.

Human life is a part of all of this. We too come, strut our stuff upon the stage of life for a little while, then go and are not seen again. As long as life seems to be like this, not more than a passing dream, it will be marked by an inherent sadness that cannot be escaped. You can deny, suppress, dissociate, keep yourself busy constantly; endlessly seek pleasure, stimulation and entertainment but you cannot escape the fact that all things will pass. You will lose everyone and everything you love until your turn will come and you too will vanish from human sight. There is no denying and no escaping from the common fate of all who live.

Yet there is hope, for the visible life in this world is just part of a much greater journey. Here is where life's meaning lies and here is where freedom is found. Love, meaning, and freedom cannot be realized while chasing goals that are limited to the small interval of time between the birth of a body and its demise. They cannot be reduced to worldly values or experiences. Their source is beyond the everyday pettiness and worries, beyond the sadness, conflict and fear that distort human life. Love and freedom are the meaning of life; they infuse life with purpose and significance. Nowhere else can authentic purpose be found; not in the endless whirl of human experience, the desires and goals of a lifetime.

Unless the desire for what is real, for the Truth of all existence, arises in your mind, you will not have the necessary interest and motivation to pursue a real enquiry into the meaning of life. This enquiry cannot be undertaken on a casual basis. The casualness of most modern thinking, its careless consideration of things from no real basis, from an over-conceptualized state of mind detached from what it considers and lost in a haze of conceptual projections, will never lead you anywhere but round and round in a circle that goes nowhere again and again. Life itself is not thinking, it is not the concepts you have about it good or bad. Life is direct, immediate; it takes place in awareness, in Being Itself without the mediation of concepts. You do not have to define pain, to describe it or examine it to know what pain is as experience. Pain, whether physical or emotional, is directly and intimately felt. No thinking or analysis is needed to recognize that you are experiencing pain. All of life is like that. You need not think about life to be alive, to understand that you exist.

It is a sad fact that too often the modern mind is unable to really live or deeply experience its own existence. The experiences of life are not met directly but are covered over by mental activity, by the constant busyness of mind that keeps itself one step removed from its own experience. Such an existence is not life; it substitutes mental activity and conceptual projections for experience itself. Running through all this activity is a kind of unspoken belief, an unconscious assumption: That one can actually understand one's own existence and the world around you through this mental haze and meaningless pseudo-detachment.

This unspoken assumption, this unconscious and unexamined bias permeates academia, scholasticism, science, indeed most areas of modern thought. While it is true a kind of objectivity is often required in the analysis and study of things, the limitations of this approach are, in general, seldom recognized or acknowledged. On the individual level we can, at least sometimes, recognize that to understand something we must experience it, penetrate it. When it comes to formal attempts to understand, however, such as through the social sciences, the bias that outside observation, though resting on unquestioned a priori assumptions, will lead to understanding usually prevails. Superficial examination is too often the order of the day and understanding that does not go beyond the surface is considered adequate and accurate.

Again it was a beautiful, warm and sunny day, a cloudless bright blue sky overhead and everywhere the scent of pine needles as the sunshine warmed the earth. By the calendar it was still the middle of winter, but spring was making her appearance and would not be denied. In the distance, the snow-covered peaks were a reminder that winter was not yet over; the rains would come again and snow too, but the day was unconcerned and would not listen. Tomorrow the winds may return, bringing with them the winter, yet today was the time to celebrate the rebirth of life. In the distance, from the bottom of the hill came the sound of the tree frogs welcoming the spring. For them it was time to come together and start once again the regeneration of life. Their song was unceasing, going on for hours, a glad refrain of many individuals coming together as one.

It was a day for recollection, for remembering the beauty that life can be. Beauty is all around us, even in the city that is so. Central to the Navajo tribe's traditional religion is the idea of beauty and harmony. I walk in beauty and beauty surrounds me is the ideal by which they try to live. How many of us walk in beauty with open eyes and a grateful heart that welcomes each new day? Or do we allow ourselves to be weighed down by our cares and worries? Do we absorb ourselves in the tasks of the day and never look up at the sky above, so open and free? Do we see the life all around us with its spontaneity and freedom, the freedom of a bird in flight winging its way across a trackless sky?

Life was not meant to be drudgery and routine, habit masquerading as existence. Yes, there is that part of life, but even here we can meet it with a song on our lips and a heart that is open and free. It is always our choice how we would greet the day; the power of choice tends to be forgotten. It seems as if the conditions of life and our responsibilities determine our happiness and limit our freedom. We may not realize that this is only a belief, and a forgetting of our ability to choose. The power of choice is always with us. Through the use or nonuse of it we determine the course of our lives. Life unfolds and develops in the direction of the choices we consistently make. We can always choose freedom no matter the apparent circumstances. The mind and heart can be free and will be free if we do not bury them in cares and worry or deny them through excessive focus on comfort and security. To be comfortable is good, to have material needs met is important, but without freedom and love, life becomes stale and meaningless.

What is the basis of your life; what gives it a foundation and meaning? What is there that you value that infuses your day to day with purpose? Or is there a purpose to what you do and how you do it? Too often is modern existence a continuous round of habit and routine repeated day after day. It may vary during the week, even change a little as the months go by, but never are you free from the deadening round of activities, from repetition, from the demands of a life dedicated to security and material prosperity. The American writer, Henry David Thoreau, once famously said, "The mass of men lead lives of quiet desperation." Is that you? Or do you lead a life of noisy desperation?

As a child I would come into the house after running around through the warm dark night for hours with my friends, playing hide and seek and other children's games. The excitement of the chase, the thick, humid darkness wrapping around me like a blanket, the cricket's song and everywhere the smell of lilacs; all this was still vividly present in my mind as I stepped into the house to find my parents watching the nightly news on television. An air of routine, the tiredness at the end of a long day of labor permeated the room; a static and dull sense of existence sat before me, tired and lifeless. I felt great pity for them, compassion for how they had to go through life. And I said to myself over and over as this scene repeated itself again and again throughout my childhood, "I will never live like this." I do not mean here to disrespect my parents; they were good people who worked hard to raise my sisters and myself and give us a good life. They gave us a religious upbringing which I also value highly though I went in somewhat of a different direction spiritually. Their life was not that different from millions of other middle-class families throughout America at that time, good hardworking people. Yet to the eyes of a child there was a vacuum, an emptiness that characterized that kind of life. It was a comfortable, somewhat secure existence, but to me it seemed like a living death.

Is this how life is for you; underneath all the continuous stimulation ever present in modern life: Television, computer, iPad, smartphone, whatever latest gimmick to get your attention someone has invented? Beyond the refrigerator full of delicious food, all the toys for both adults and children, the shiny automobiles outside your door, the busy schedule and constant attempts at secondhand communication, despite the drugs legal and illegal you may consume, the fine wines and quality beers on your table; does life seem meaningful to you? Do you have a sense of purpose that transcends or perhaps gives meaning to the daily routine? Is there a point to or good reason for all you are doing? Do you rise each morning, happy to greet the new day with joy in your heart? Or are you living the modern equivalent of a life of quiet desperation, keeping as busy as possible so you won't notice, keeping all the balls in the air like a juggler so you won't have to look down and see where you are standing?

What could be the basis of a fair, equitable, and just economy? Could it be the principle of enough for all, the meeting of the basic needs of all citizens before permitting the accumulation of excess wealth by the few? Would it not include the responsibility for each to participate in a meaningful manner, to perform some work or service for the whole? And would not such a system take care of the helpless, the children and the elderly, the disabled and the sick?

Our present economic system has these ideas as some part of its goals yet unfortunately often falls short. Perhaps the most glaring discrepancy is the enthronement of the accumulation of wealth as an ideal to be admired and a goal to be reached. People of great wealth, especially those who are self-made, rising from humble circumstances, become celebrities who are greatly honored by the media and almost worshipped by some or so it seems. Always the powerful and famous occupy the highest niche in our society: The generals, successful businesspeople, artists of all kinds who have attained prominence in their art, professional athletes, politicians; all who have been highly successful in their chosen field of endeavor. We seem as a society to worship power and success. This is almost too obvious to need mentioning yet it is often the most obvious that is examined the least. For me this brings up an important question: Why idolize the impermanent and temporary?

The great heroes and success stories of my childhood are all gone, buried beneath the sands of time. For some, their accomplishments may live on such as great art or perhaps the businesses that were created. Even then, how long does anything last in this world? So often what is here today will be gone tomorrow no matter what we do. The winds of change blow ceaselessly; in the end nothing can withstand them for long. All things pass away; only the sky and the earth endure as an old proverb says. So the question remains: Why worship success and its creations when they are so obviously fleeting and impermanent?

Could the reason have something to do with our own sense of mortality? Do these individuals and their accomplishments seem somehow larger than life, do they represent triumph over the uncertainties we all face, transcendence of impermanence? They may also represent for many the kind of life they would like to lead: Glamorous, financially well-off with all the material comforts, stimulations, and pleasures. Does it make sense to emulate and admire what is subject to decay and dissolution? Does it profit you to gain the whole world and yet lose your connection to your own soul?

There is something here in life that is worthy of your admiration and respect. You will not find it through the idolization of something or someone outside of yourself. It will not be found through the pursuit of wealth, or fame or even the attainment thereof. Your ultimate destiny does not lie within the limits of this world, its honors or achievements. All things will wither, decay and pass away; the glorious Reality within you, which is the basis and cause of your life, will not perish. Perhaps it's time to begin to acquaint yourself with That whose value cannot be measured.

The moon was shining in the west, not yet a full sphere but more than a sliver. It was a crescent in the western sky, shedding a gentle light on the darkened earth. As always the pine trees stood tall and unbending, their dark shapes reaching toward the stars. Sometimes the darkness is like an old friend come to visit the earth and envelop all in its peaceful embrace. The beauty of the night has been lost to those who live in the cities surrounded by the harsh glare of artificial light. The stars cannot be seen, even the moon's delicate beauty is lessened by competition from the towers of glass and steel and the blinking traffic lights that direct the busy traffic of the night. We are always on the move, we children of a mechanized, noisy society. Always restless, always seeking we know not what, and filling that unknowing, the emptiness that haunts us from within, with entertainments and pleasures that don't last and with the many things we buy that bring no real satisfaction.

The zombies that appear on our movie screens and televisions are perhaps a good metaphor for what life is becoming. Lifeless creatures that nonetheless are always on the move, trying to find life that they might devour it. They are unaware of their plight, their actual condition, but are driven by it to enact a parody of life devouring itself.

What do I mean by reason? I will start by addressing what is unreasonable. Surely it is unreasonable to live in a way that contradicts and conflicts with our basic nature. Can it be anything but unreasonable to live in a self-destructive manner whether individually or collectively as a society? Our way of life is very destructive to the earth on which we live and her natural systems that are the basis for life as we know it. It seems unreasonable to me and many others to pursue life in a manner that destroys the very ground beneath our feet.

To address life in the individual sense, is it reasonable to spend all our time and energy devoted to what is superficial and ignore the depth and breadth of our Mind and Being from which life itself springs and in which all meaning is found? Does the image of yourself as nothing but a smart monkey with clothes on, an ape with tennis shoes and a computer, which is the view of scientific materialism and our modern secular society – does this picture of yourself seem adequate or satisfying or complete? Is it reasonable? Does it adequately account for the richness of life and experience? Is a life devoted to being a consumer of things and services, a life devoted to the acquisition of more and more toys, a life spent in pursuit of pleasure and stimulation of all kinds, of escape from and avoidance of all that is deemed unpleasant or uncomfortable – does such a life seem reasonable or complete to you?

Perhaps it is time to question the modern way of life, the attitudes and understanding that characterize it, and its effects on ourselves individually, on society as a whole and on the earth itself. Even a cursory but honest examination of the present situation in the world, in our society, and in the lives of many individuals, reveals the lack of reason as a guiding principle or source of motivation for what we do.

What do I mean by reason? To act reasonably is to act in our own best interest at the minimum. To not act self-destructively or in a way that inflicts lasting or irreparable damage on that on which our lives depend. To work together with others in a way that leads to a fair and equitable life for all. To live from that place which is highest in us, from the position of love, goodwill and helpfulness towards our fellow human beings without exception. To not cherish hatred, envy, grievances and anger, but to practice forgiveness and tolerance towards all. To respect our differences yet not make of them a cause for conflict and division. To recognize we are all children of the One Creator, the One Great Mystery who loves us all equally. To recognize the meaning of life is not found in isolation and separation, in selfishness or pettiness, but in joining with each other in a spirit of love and cooperation. And finally, to live from an attitude informed by reason is to take full responsibility for our thoughts, emotions and actions; to cease projecting blame onto others, and to make a concerted effort to be kind and fair to each other in all circumstances.

The day is almost over, the sun low in the west. It was a beautiful warm day, the sky a pale blue and slightly overcast, the sun bright yet gentle. The rains have stopped for now and everywhere the grass is poking up through the leaves and pine needles, bright green shoots reaching for the sun. Spring is still a month away yet life has begun to regenerate itself with the help of the moist earth and the gentle sunshine. How mysterious is this continuous process of birth, growth, reproduction, degeneration and death. It transcends the individual forms the way the forest transcends its individual trees. Trees die but the forest goes on.

We are a part of all this, in a different way perhaps, yet still a part. As the body we are subject to the same processes as all living things. As self-awareness, we transcend the body, extending beyond the merely physical. Narrowly identified as a body, our life is tied to the earth, limited to the senses, and we seem to be condemned to trudge wearily along, one among many traversing the dusty roads that lead from birth to death. In between there are pleasures and diversions, fleeting perhaps but available to those who would pursue them. Distractions come and go like the seasons, like the natural cycles, but all pleasures, all stimulations are ephemeral at best, here one day, gone the next. Nothing on this earth is permanent, unchanging. All things pass away; even the highest mountains will be gone someday, leaving only pebbles and sand where they once stood. It has been well said that the only thing permanent in this world is change.

There is another dimension to all this; one that transcends the superficiality of the physical and its mental and emotional preoccupations. This dimension contains the depths and the heights that lie beyond the merely obvious, beyond the outer level of form. In our current way of living with its preoccupation with personal fulfillment and self-expression, the subtle and universal is overlooked in the headlong rush to find what is pleasing and stimulating to the ego. The Truth does not lend Itself to the ego's aims. It cannot be used for personal gain and satisfaction. Truth lies forever outside the domain of worldly goals and accomplishments, beyond the reach of the ego and its desires.

If you would find this Existence, this Beingness from which your life arises, you must slow down and reevaluate everything you do and think and feel. The process of returning to Essence is not casual or careless or halfhearted. It is not one among many other things you are doing or the one that takes place on weekends when you read books or attend workshops. These activities can be included, can be a part of the journey but only that. To return to the Source of your Being requires a lifelong commitment, a single higher purpose to which your life and everything that is part of it is consecrated.

The rains did not come although they have been promised and predicted. The sky is gray and there have been a few brief sprinkles. The forest is drying out, more rain is needed here and more snow in the high country. Water is truly precious, without it nothing can live be it plant, animal, or human. We take it for granted as we take everything for granted that Mother Earth and life provide us. Society and most of us as individuals forget to be grateful for what we are so freely given. Our ingratitude is killing the earth and may well lead to our demise unless we become willing to change. Without gratitude there is no appreciation; what you do not appreciate you do not value and take care of. What is not taken care of degrades over time.

Surely it is madness to neglect our responsibility to the earth and the natural systems that sustain and make possible our existence. Could we say that the attitude, the active position of refusing to take responsibility for actions and their effects is too often characteristic of the human mind on the level of the individual? That too often our self-centeredness overrides our sense of responsibility? Is it then any wonder why this attitude prevails on the greater level of society, the nation? What is society but a collection of individuals and all their traits good and bad? What is problem enough on the individual level is positively tragic when magnified to the position of the whole society where responsibility is much easier to evade or deny. When an economic entity such as a small business or a large corporation damages the environment in which we live, we are all nonetheless responsible, for we reap the benefits of economic activity and the technology it produces, each and every one of us.

There is no time left to undo the damage that has been done, to restore balance and stability to our Mother Earth. Though at the time of this writing, an economic slowdown prevails in much of the world's economy, what this means in practical terms is a slowdown in the rate of damage inflicted on nature, not a cessation. Indeed, the modern economy on which our societies depend must keep going and growing to meet our basic needs. It will not be made to stop or to change for this is unthinkable to the powers that drive it and control governments. And, to be honest, to completely change the way we live is also unthinkable to most. We are literally caught in a trap of our own making, a trap that has many facets and many parts but no exit.

History is replete with examples of times like ours; times in which eras are ending and empires fading away. At such a time life changes dramatically for all no matter what level of society they inhabit. Rich and poor, the powerful and the powerless; no one is unaffected by the changes and turmoil that are a part of it.

There are some important differences, however, between today and those times past. Never has the entire world been so interconnected and interdependent economically. Never in the past has the population even approached today's number of close to seven billion. Never has so much of the natural world been degraded, destabilized and polluted. As wars are a not uncommon feature or cause of the end of empires and eras, never has mankind had so much destructive power at its disposal as today; enough power to destroy the world as we know it and bring an end to most of the life upon it including humanity itself. And never before, when faced with the collapse of transportation systems and the infrastructure that supports our lives, have so many people been living with no connection to the natural world and the simplicity of life. Raised in an artificial environment, mentally and emotionally divorced from everything natural, taught to think of nature as simply a source for the raw materials needed to live our artificial lives, and feeling completely justified to take, extract, and remove what we need no matter the destruction involved, the possibility of adapting to the extreme changes coming seems quite remote for many of us. The centralization of human population in very large congested cities is not sustainable, yet where are all their inhabitants to go practically speaking? I do not know the answer nor does anyone else.

What is an economy? What is involved in the making and supporting of what we call our economy? The classical definition of an economy has to do with the production and exchange of goods and services. The science of economics, sometimes referred to as the dismal science, seems to regard economic activity as if it takes place in a vacuum. Economists do not fundamentally consider or factor in the background, the context in which this activity takes place. Thus modern economics, completely abstracted from the natural world that makes it possible, is able to ignore the damage that is being done to the earth unless that damage affects profits. This view, conscious or unconscious, underlies our modern economic system and the thinking that has created and perpetuates it. It's as if an economist, when he goes on a picnic, sees only the value of the picnic basket and the food it carries. He doesn't notice the blue sky, the warm sunshine, the beautiful natural setting, and the little stream running beside the picnic grounds. Yet all of these contribute to and make the experience of going on a picnic what it is. Without them, it is not a picnic. This is but a superficial example, however, that does not do justice to the degree our blindness to nature pervades our economy and the premises on which it is established.

Does the blue sky above notice our coming and going? A body is born, matures and develops, ages, declines and dies. The mind or soul that seems to inhabit it: where does it come from and where does it go? The modern consensus view of reality that reduces identity to nothing but the body itself is but another egoic delusion, an attempt to control life to its own satisfaction by denying the existence of a higher power or higher laws that exist beyond the ego's control or belief system. The modern view is simply one belief system among many that have appeared over the course of human history. Unlike virtually all the others, however, it does not recognize an aspect or dimension of existence that transcends or is not limited to the physical. Actually, the belief system of materialism was first advanced thousands of years ago by philosophical schools of thought in both the East and West. It did not flourish in either case due to its rejection by the great majority of thinkers and its obvious reductionism that did not suffice to adequately explain the broad spectrum of humanity's life experience.

In this world all things arise, flourish for awhile, then disappear again as a result of natural processes. That is as true for mountains and rivers as for living things like humans and giraffes. The impermanence of visible life is or can be taken as grounds for a sense of urgency regarding the essential question that is posed to every being that is self-aware by the very fact of its existence: what or who am I and what is the purpose of my existence? Looking at history, there seems to have always been a tendency for many to ignore, to default on this question and busy themselves with the details of everyday life, to become preoccupied with what is obvious and visible and base life on this preoccupation. Never has this tendency been more pronounced than at the present time, and it seems to me an obvious rationalization of our modern mindset to justify our fixation on consumption, pleasure, stimulation, and escape from responsibility, by claiming that nothing exists other than what we busy ourselves with. This is not simply a default but a denial of the question itself and its replacement with meaninglessness.

The fixation on the obvious is accompanied by a surprising denial of the obvious in another way. The one fact of our existence that is equally true for everyone and inevitable is that it will come to an end. Death waits for all men and for all women too. This inescapable fact of our existence puts a limit on our activities, goals, attainments, honors and pleasures. It brings all things to an end, making a mockery of our pretensions and self-importance. The king and the peasant, the rich man and the beggar, the genius and the fool; all will lie beside each other, all distinctions erased, on the common ground of death. Death will embrace each in turn and life will vanish into that unknown territory that lies beyond our sight.

Sometimes when I enter the forest I feel its silent reproach. Not condemnation or hostility for what we have done, no grievance or deep-seated animosity, just a gentle reproach for the destruction we have caused. The big trees are long gone, cut down every one. The forest grew back then was cut down again. Today we are a little less destructive than formerly, tending to manage rather than simply destroy. So we have forests again to walk through and enjoy though they are but a pale semblance of the majesty and beauty of the past.

Trees have such dignity and presence. They give shade to all and share their seeds freely with the birds and the squirrels asking nothing in return. They die silently, without a complaint, yielding their bodies to the chainsaw and the sawmill unlike we human beings who go out kicking and screaming, moaning, "Why me?" Indeed, why not me? All things born must die for all bodies are temporary no matter how long lived. One year or three thousand years, it does not matter, the end is certain. Death always keeps his appointments; his appointment book is always full. And yet death is only the end of a chapter and the beginning of the next one. The body will last as long as it is useful. When its usefulness is gone, why hang on to it? Life in this world is a pilgrimage, no more, no less.

There is a way to make life meaningful, to enter into a relationship with all living things and nature that make life possible. This cannot be done from the perspective of separation; the separative and mechanical theory of life reduces all living things to mere physical objects, deals only with the superficial, and denies their wholeness and true interdependence. Balance cannot be restored while the deep and beautiful mystery that is life is ignored and disrespected, replaced with a model in which bits and pieces of nature are plugged back into the holes left by their absence due to human activity. We have not only upset the equilibrium of the natural world by destroying some of the species that are a part of the great web of life and changed the environment in destructive ways; modern humanity has almost completely lost the sense of the wholeness of the natural order and our place within it, as part of it.

The river is running very fast here as the dam is just a couple hundred yards upstream. Released from its confinement, it is rushing towards freedom, flowing back into its natural bed, rejoicing once again. Bringing water to the sacred desert, the river's banks are lined with ancient trees, a bright green border that contrasts with the sand-colored hills and cliffs around it and the bare, rocky mountains lining the horizon on the other side.

All rivers are sacred. We have recognized this since the earliest days of civilization and before. The rivers bring life-giving waters to the plains and deserts, the low country where it is most needed to sustain our agriculture and our life. We have used rivers, dammed them, worshipped them, and now we are polluting them like never before. Few rivers run clear and clean as in the old days and our gratitude has been replaced by indifference and a lack of respect.

At this critical time in the history of the human race, it may be already too late to change course. In that case, the momentum of events may override our human ability to control them and we will have to learn how to respond creatively. This will include the necessity to join together, to correct the tendency to isolate. It will be necessary to overcome fear and selfishness and work together locally for the common good.

There is no more time to waste, no time to chase after the ephemeral pleasures of a world about to vanish. What would you do if you realized your house was on fire? Would you ignore that fact and go on planning your next party or would you respond appropriately to the fire, the situation at hand? The party is over though the guests have not realized it yet. The table may be piled high with food, the wine and beer still flowing; outside a massive fire is approaching and there is no stopping a fire that was set long ago and fed with fuel until it has become huge and is burning everywhere. There is no place where you can run and hide. All of us will have to stand and face the consequences of our actions though the day of reckoning has been long delayed.

Unfortunately, the mechanism of denial so ever present in human affairs continues to operate even as the world around us undergoes its accelerating upheavals. The time is fast coming when denial will no longer be able to keep from your vision the sight of the Four Horsemen of the Apocalypse coming over the horizon. Nothing can stop them at this time from sweeping across the face of the earth, leaving our present civilization much reduced. In places it may be reduced to rubble, elsewhere a semblance of order may remain. All will depend on the spiritual maturity of the inhabitants. Where an attitude of tolerance, forgiveness, and mutual helpfulness prevails, order can be maintained and the organization of life will be adequate to meet human needs. What will be needed most of all is a willingness to join together regardless of our human differences in pursuit of a common goal. This requires the recognition of a common interest that all share.

It has been raining heavily off and on for three days. The holy mountain is shrouded in cloud. Except for an occasional glimpse of its snow-covered peaks, it remains in solitude, protected by its cloud covering. Higher up on the mountain, the ground is covered with snow. The manzanita bushes with their new green leaves hold themselves above the snow, waiting for the return of the sun. It's unusual to have so much rain at this time of year though it is good for the trees and other living things.

What is mind? Mind is that by which you are aware, aware of your existence (self-awareness), aware of the context in which your existence seems to be embedded and of which you seem to be a part. Is there self-existence if you are not aware of it? Certainly not in the human sense. Existence without awareness of it is not possible, for mind is fundamentally endowed with awareness of itself. All that truly exists has the attribute of being aware and is aware that it is aware. Without this, there is no existence for life itself, Being itself, takes place in Mind. The world you think you see is nothing but your mind, and the figures and forms that appear as if outside of you are your projections, nothing else. They have the seeming reality and the ability to affect you that you gave them. This is true of everyone without exception.

All is One, everything a whole part of the One Unity that is Mind, that is all and contains all. The dream of separation is but a jumble of appearances, figures seemingly disconnected from one another, aimlessly wandering about, giving imaginary meaning to what they do and what they see. As these figures seem to be something other than mind, mind itself is then relegated to a secondary role, believed to be a byproduct of processes that are other than mind. Processes that somehow give rise to mind, a phenomenon that is completely different from its supposed source in its nature and its functioning. To think thusly is to believe in nonsense.

The holy mountain looms over the small town like a great protector. Its vast and benevolent presence can be felt everywhere by those who are sensitive. Life goes on here as usual. Shops open, shops close, people buy what they need and what they don't need, and always the constant stream of automobiles darting here and there. Yet nothing can disturb the peace of the mountain, not the noise and restlessness of those who live in its shadow, not their indifference nor the chaotic conditions of their lives. The holy mountain does not judge or condemn. Its peace is offered to all and its beauty is freely shared. You need only look up with an open mind and heart free of the deadening effect of the past, free of expectation and evaluation. Then beauty itself can embrace you and show you what lies beyond the reach of the mind that is preoccupied with itself and its petty desires.

What is impossible to do is what you must do. Because it is impossible of accomplishment, it has nothing to do with a self, an ego, whose orientation is towards doing something, accomplishing something. The ego operates with the motivation to attain; it sets goals and directs effort and planning to reach its goals. The only goal worth pursuing is the goal you cannot reach because the "you," the self you think you are, is the denial of that goal and will obstruct its attainment every step of the way. Yet the self must be used. By purifying it and dedicating its service to a higher purpose, the self can be used to go beyond itself. In the end, however, the self does not reach the goal for the attainment of Reality is the disappearance of a sense of "self" and the revealing of your true nature, the Self or spiritual nature, as what you are.

The mighty caravan
Sails across the desert.
Knocking on your stateroom door
A dervish, wild-eyed, disheveled,
Tells you dinner is being served
At the oasis.
Then he lops off your head

And throws it onto the sand.
Leave it there, you don't need it.
Enjoy the meal and the coolness
Under the palm trees.
When he brings you your head
Let him put it on.
If it doesn't fit, leave it there,
You will be given another one
That is better than the first
Until you don't need a head.
The sky will be your head
And emptiness your home.

* * *

Be prepared to be alone
There is no one here but you.
Many forms, shapes and sizes
Like a merry-go-round
Always moving, spinning. Stop and
You will discover Disneyland
Is but a desert inhabited by shadows
That seem to walk and talk
And move about.
Give up your life among shadows,
Become life itself, let the inner Sun
Shine brightly till all shadows disappear.
Dance with that sun and
The darkness of night will not touch you.

For you shall know the Truth, and the Truth shall make you free.
Jesus of Nazareth

Chapter 4

The Same Thing

What is the use of doing the same thing over and over, walking the same path every day, your eyes fixed on the ground or staring blankly ahead, never looking at the bright blue sky above, never listening to the joyful song of the birds who share this world with you? The birds will never get a promotion, or buy a new car, or go on that dream vacation; yet their song expresses the joy of life just as it is. The many accretions we have added to life, all the layers of comfort and ambition and pleasure obstruct the meaning and joy of living just as a dark cloud blots out the sun. Yes, certain conditions must be met: Food, shelter, clothing, a chance to give and receive love, and hopefully meaningful work though most work can be experienced as meaningful if that be your choice.

There was a man who once looked at the Sun without blinking, without flinching. The Sun asked him what he was doing and he replied, "I want to see if you are as bright as everyone says you are."

"What do they know of brightness," the Sun replied. "When do they lift their eyes from the things of this world and notice the sky? The darkest night is not a condition of my absence; it is a state of mind that wills not to notice the light all around, to ignore the great mystery in which everything is enveloped. It is as if once noticing you are on a ship sailing the great ocean, you decide never to look at the ocean again though it carries you to your destination. A journey of many years and many steps becomes a small circle going nowhere."

"Easy for you to say," replied the man. "Your path is set high in the heavens, far above the confusion and strife casting their shadows across the life of humanity."

"Everything is a choice," said the Sun, "and the choice is always yours; never is choice denied you. Some choose to soar across the sky like the eagle, to shatter the chains that bind humanity to a destiny of dust and decay. To fly is not easy, but it is necessary and lies within the reach of everyone if they but make the effort. The caterpillar plodding along, slow but determined, does what it is meant to do until it has fulfilled its responsibility. Then is it ready to receive the Grace that is waiting when it emerges from its solitude. A thing of beauty and freedom, it flies away on the wings of Love and becomes Grace Itself."

The desert is an appropriate metaphor for life. In the heat of summer it can become dry and barren, its inhabitants holding on till come the life-giving rains. Everything then comes alive again. Green, the color of life, returns and blankets the earth with grasses. Flowers emerge on the hardy bushes that dot the landscape, usually yellow, sometimes white or even violet. The leaves fill out and everything begins to feel good about itself again. Desert creatures are widely varied by habit, appearance, attitude, diet and size. Some are rather prickly like the scorpion that is easily aroused to defense or attack. The cottontail rabbit is shy, easily startled, and quick to take flight; the desert fox, also shy, is yet clever, always ready when a prospective meal presents itself. The roadrunner, that unlikely bird who has forgotten how to fly, is always on the move, always looking for where its next meal is coming from and ready to flee at a moment's notice. And the coyote, the king of the hill until the desert wolf appears, alternates between rest in the heat of the day and constant motion in the night and early morning.

Always on the lookout for food and alert to any sign of danger, the coyote has born the full brunt of modern man's hatred of nature and the wild creatures who live their life indifferent to our needs and wants and values. For more than a century, it has been trapped, poisoned, and shot whenever possible yet has thrived and expanded its range to most of the country, even where it was not found before modern civilization arrived. Unlike the bison, the passenger pigeon and others, God's dog, as it is called by some native tribes, has refused to go quietly into that good night, to disappear into oblivion like so many other good creatures. Perhaps the coyote still has something to teach us or to learn before it shuffles off into the unknown. Life is born, flourishes for awhile, then disappears, its forms of expression changing, vanishing, reborn as other forms. The life behind and in all forms does not die, the essence is beyond life and death, change and decay. This is true of all.

How does life arise in the midst of death? Is death the end; does it conquer life or does life leave death behind to lay in the dust while life itself starts another chapter of the never-ending story that unfolds in time? Life is both of time and out of time. Its origin is the Eternal, the deathless, yet it plays on through the masquerades of time, putting on one mask after another, discarding them when their usefulness is over. Life is not the mask but that which animates the mask that the play, the parade of dream figures, may go on until everyone tires of dreaming, of pretending, of playing a role devoid of lasting meaning. The play will not end until everyone, even to the last, has lost the desire to play at life and chosen instead to be life itself.

When did the ideas arise that underlie modern "civilization"? Was the greedy restlessness that torments the heart and drives the mind always a part of us or did it appear somewhere along the way we have come, and grow and flourish until it attained its full flowering in the modern era? As Carl Jung, the Swiss psychoanalyst, pointed out long ago, Western humanity would not rest until the entire world was infected by this uneasy and greedy approach to living, and the passage of time has borne out the truth of his observation. Now that the entire world has to some extent or another subscribed to the modern Western belief in the unquestioned rightness of technological "progress," unceasing economic growth and unrestrained development, we see the results everywhere. Why change a winning strategy unless, of course, winning turns out to be losing.

The Life within all
Is not a passing fancy,
Not the ephemeral stuff of which
All dreams are made.
All forms of clay
Last only for a moment.
When a clay pot shatters
Is the space within it affected?
Life is the within of things
Its true content, the context
In which all arises.

Let all rest within Being
Without number or difference.
Form is an idle fancy
Driven by the winds of desire.
Never does the wind cease to scatter
The leaves that lie upon the road.
Don't be as a dead leaf, dry and shriveled,
Dancing in the dust
Victim of its own imaginings.
Be the tree, the roots, and the sky.
Ignore the death that dances all around you
And be life's laughing and happy face
Which sees not death but the changeless
In the midst of change.

* * *

Cross, Crescent, and Menorah,
Symbols of an unspoken idea

That of which we cannot speak.
No symbol or concept
Can touch the infinite depth
That cannot be measured.
A depth without high or low,
No direction, no time or space.
The universe is the thinnest of skins
Stretched across the Real,
Concealing what cannot be seen
But must be known by that
Which transcends the intellect.
No identity, no history, no thought
No past or future, no good or bad
Neither acceptance nor rejection
Will bring you face to face
With the unknown.
You are that
Through which It knows Itself.

What is knowledge, what is it to know something? Is knowledge mere perception? I perceive an object in my field of vision and in or as the act of perceiving, of seeing, do I know it? Or do I simply know something is there before me, an object with shape, color, size, and perhaps other attributes; a thing to which I have given a name or, more to the point, an object which I was taught to label with a certain name. A tree, a house, a street, a dog, all objects of perception with whom I have a kind of relationship and about which I may have certain ideas, value judgments, likes and dislikes. I may have experiences with and memories of those experiences with any object of perception; experiences that may be considered good or bad. When you thus see something in particular, an object of past experience, do you really see it, do you "know" it, or do you just see its form and simultaneously does the effect of your past experiences with this thing before you condition and shape the quality of your perception and your mind's reaction to it? Perception inevitably involves a sorting out, a categorizing and interpretation of the sense data that appears in your mind. This automatic activity is based on the past, i.e. what you have been taught and what you have experienced. And remember, perception is an activity of consciousness, of awareness, of mind. Mind is never a blank slate on which perception records its experience but is rather an ever active and dynamic activity, a process which receives, interacts with, and interprets what appears in awareness.

In the light of all this activity and the subsequent conditioning of the mind and its interaction with perception, can we say that the act of knowing something is independent of the act of perception? I think not. So again arises the question, what exactly is it to know something? I think that knowledge or knowing can be divided into two aspects. The first is the knowing associated with the "outer" action of perception, with the whole array of experience associated with the world that seems to be "outside" our mind.

The second kind of knowing is associated with the activity of inner perception. This is the perception which is a kind of inner hearing of thoughts, an inner seeing of images, and an inner perception of feelings; physical feelings in the body, the storm of emotional feelings such as anger, fear etc., and feeling states of mind and body. The human mind does not simply think and feel, it is aware of its thoughts and feelings. Mind is most fundamentally awareness, consciousness itself. All the functions of mind take place in awareness, in a context or background of awareness itself without which we would be unaware of them. So what is this inner knowing? In a manner analogous to the outer knowing, we know or are aware of the inner activity of mind through perception, a kind of perception that is turned inward and hears, sees, and feels the inner content of mind.

Yet there is another kind of knowing. This knowing is

associated with belief, with understanding, with the opinions we hold about things. Here we are dealing with more abstract and purely mental aspects of mind that are somewhat removed from the simple act of perception though they still rest upon it. This is the realm of reasoning and contemplation. The mind is moved to focus on a certain thought, a theme or subject or observation, directing the thinking process to concentrate upon it for a purpose. Beliefs, conscious and unconscious, values, previous opinions, biases; all these play a role and impinge upon the thinking process, almost inevitably influencing the result. If we would associate knowing with some significant degree of accuracy regarding what is known, then it is obvious that the thinking process itself, the consideration and weighing of the theme and all its aspects, should best be clear, open, and as minimally distorted as possible by previously held ideas, opinions and biases.

Ask yourself truthfully, how often is this the case for me or for others? Opinions tend to crystallize around value judgments, around what is considered most important, as well as strongly-held ideas of good and bad. Often, if one looks at a particular issue from both sides, carefully examining the arguments and reasoning involved, there will appear to be a certain consistency in the approach from either side and an attempt to be reasonable, i.e. to use reason to make the case for their position. Yet often diametrically different conclusions are reached about the same issue. Clearly, generally speaking, human reasoning does not often lead to a simple and direct understanding that could be described as actual knowing, i.e. accurate knowledge of an issue that stands beyond opinion and bias. What is so often believed to be knowledge about something is usually no more than disguised and strongly-held opinion. This brings us back to the original question: What exactly is knowing, to know something? Surely it is something other than mere opinion based on differing judgments of value, of good or bad. Knowing, if there is such a thing, must stand beyond varying interpretations, opinions, fantasies, projections, beyond all the activity of the human mind whose purpose is to find some certainty that aligns with what we want to believe.

To know something is to experience it directly, beyond mental activity and its contradictions. We know it through awareness itself prior to mental or emotional intervention and reaction. Knowing, most simply and directly, begins with the basic fact of our existence. We know that we exist. We know by virtue of the fact that we are aware, self-aware of our existence, of our Being. From there we become aware of our mind's activity (Descartes' famous dictum: I think, therefore I am), thought, feelings etc. Somewhere in there also arises the awareness of perceptions both inner and outer without which we would not know we have thoughts and feelings. Is it possible to know the perceptual phenomena of life in the same direct, completely self-referential way that we know our own existence? I think not.

Do objects arise out there separate from the one who is aware of them, who perceives them? Or do they arise in minds, your mind and my mind as one mind, as a mutual act of perception and recognition? What is it to perceive and to be perceived? Do subject and object arise together or independently? Does the existence of each depend on the other, a mutually dependent act of existence in which both appear simultaneously?

I look and I see
Who is seeing what?
How do I know that I see?
How do I know what I see?
The past determines the present,
The present creates the future,
The past determines and creates the future.
The future becomes the present
Then the past.

Where does knowing fit in to all this?
I know that I am
I know that you are
I do not know what you are.
All see the same thing
But yet see differently.
Each thing appears differently
According to who perceives it.
What then are we perceiving?
Does the thing in itself exist
Independent of all who might perceive it,
Independent of all perceptual difference?
Can the question of how I know
What I know be answered
Or do I know just by being aware?
Is simple, direct knowing just a quality,
A recognition that is part of awareness itself?
Can knowing exist beyond the simple action
Of being aware?
Is it possible to even know anything
Beyond our Self Awareness?
Can I ever know what anything is,
What it is in itself?
What it is beyond perception of any kind?
Is there any such thing
As truly objective knowing?
Can any subject be truly objective
In the act of perception
If perception itself includes
Sorting out, categorizing, and interpreting
What is perceived, what is seen?
Can anything be truly seen
As it is right now
If the action of perception

Is always affected by, even based on
Past experience which forms the basis
Of sorting out and interpreting?
Thus can I ever really know
What anything is, what it is now?
Can I ever know anything beyond
The fact that I exist?
I may know objects of perception
Exist or seem to exist
But what are they really?
What anything is in itself
Must always elude my knowing,
My understanding, if that knowing
Rests on the act of perception.

* * *

Just as the sun rises in the morning
All over the world
So does the Spiritual Sun arise
In the hearts and minds of all.
The sun rises in America
In Ethiopia, India, Australia,
The same sun, the same rising
In each place at its appointed time.
Do not hinder its arising,
Closed eyes see nothing
But the darkness before them.
Dreamers see an entire world surrounding them.
Figures come and go, speak and are silent.
Many things seem to happen in dreams,
Some good, some bad, suffering
Accorded each according to desire.
The world of dreams is nothing in itself,

Not good, not bad, simply meaningless.
Do not flee nor embrace what happens.
Let it be, see it for what it is.
Let the spiritual eye be open
The single eye of Mind and Heart.
See beyond the forms of appearance,
Apparitions all, empty, void,
Unnecessary yet appropriate, each to its role
Playing it perfectly in your life.
No requiring to accept,
No requiring to reject,
The only requirements: clarity and love.
Love embraces all through the clarity of recognition.
What is real and true
Must be recognized as such.
What is illusory and meaningless
Must be discarded.
Surrounded by illusory figures and events,
Respond helpfully, not absorbed or deluded therein.
There is a place in your mind
Where delusion cannot enter.
Live in that place, act from there
And you will not be lost
In idle dreaming nor chasing shadows
That are not there.
Your mind contains all
You can see or imagine.
Maintained by thought, the dream lives on
Filling your life with the unnecessary.
Learn to recognize the difference
And discard the unnecessary that
The real and necessary may return.

He used to come frequently to all the houses in the neighborhood, asking if there were any old rags that were no longer needed. These were gratefully accepted and thrown onto the old cart he was riding. Sometimes the woman of the house would offer him an item of food such as a piece of bread with butter or a small bowl of leftovers. These were also gratefully received and stored on the cart right beside his seat. The man was very old but with a quiet strength and dignity about him. In appearance he was a rag picker, in essence clearly much more. I don't know how but even as small children some of us were able to perceive the inner worth of the man. Perhaps we were still too young to have the aliveness and freshness of our perceptions dulled by training and habit; our minds had not yet taken on the habitual and self-protective dullness of the adult world.

One day there was an accident in the neighborhood. Two cars had collided at an intersection; one driver had been injured. He was sitting on the grass beside the road with his head in his hands, his face bloody. The rag man happened to come along right about then and saw the injured man who was waiting for an ambulance as one of the bystanders had made the call for him. The rag man stopped his cart, got down and went to sit beside the injured man. He began to speak quietly as the man listened. As time went on the injured man appeared to relax more and more and seemed to be feeling better and recovering his strength. He had appeared to be in a sort of state of shock as the result of the accident, but by the time an ambulance arrived, he seemed to be feeling much better as he stood up and walked to the ambulance after a brief exchange with the rag man whom he thanked warmly.

After the ambulance drove away, a bystander asked the rag man what he had said that had so positively affected the accident victim. The rag man replied in a soft and gentle voice, "What I said was not important. It was the sympathy in my voice and the simple act of joining with him in this situation, of being willing to help, to share the pain, that helped bring him back to himself." Then he got back on his cart and continued his journey through the streets and alleys collecting old rags.

Of all the people in the neighborhood, a middle-class neighborhood where each owned the house they lived in, had all the comforts of life, and a car etc.: it was the poorest man of all, a man who clearly had very little who nonetheless gave the most. He alone was willing and able to give sympathy, love, and a helping hand to a fellow human being in need.

It's not the clothes we wear, our appearance, our possessions and social position, or our function where our simple humanity can be found. In the heart of each of us abides the kindness, sympathy, and willingness to help that represents our true being and worth. The extent to which each of us has found that, and lives from that place, determines whether we have lived a worthy life.

> If you see your brother standing on the road
> And you just pass him by
> You will not see what he has to give.
> Jesus came knocking on my door
> Dressed in rags and bleeding.
> My food and clothing he refused saying,
> "It is not these things I ask of you.
> Your heart is what I value."
> "Lord, how can I give my heart?" I replied.
> "Love me in your brothers and serve them,
> help them, forgive them all.
> Close your heart to no one
> And you will be loving me," he said.
>
> Christ looks at you through the eyes
> Of everyone you meet.
> Their need is his need.
> In a world where love

Is not given freely
We must give to all.
The beggar offers you heaven,
The thief, redemption.
All will be together in paradise.

* * *

Business is good, intoxicants very popular.
Inebriation is a pleasant state
While it lasts.
The mind dazzled by shiny toys
Buys trinkets to hang on the body.
Adorns it with fine clothing,
Colors it with rouge and lip gloss.
Quick! Before it becomes a corpse.
All will pass away in the end.
An empty space at the dinner table,
Silence where once was laughter.
Be grateful for those you love,
They are given you for a little while.
Laughter leads to tears,
Tears end in laughter.
See who waits for you
At the end of the road.
Do not fear his embrace.

Fluffy, white clouds sail slowly across the sky, a contrast to the deep blue all around them. Their seeming softness is gentle, inviting, the constantly changing shapes like a play set across the backdrop of the sky, much like the play that takes place below. A play within a play. "All the world's a stage and we are but players on it," said the Bard hundreds of years ago. As true now as then, as it has always been. "The play's the thing."

The travails of earthly life, the conflict and suffering, are all a part of the script which we have written and continue to write. Each chooses the part he/she would play and assigns roles to the others who appear in our play. When the others do not live up to the roles we have given them, we project judgment and anger upon them and attack them because we cannot control them; they will not act the way we want, they will not fulfill our expectations. If you really take the time to look at this whole dynamic honestly and deeply, you will recognize that no one can possibly fulfill your expectations just as you cannot possibly fulfill the expectations anyone has of you. Eventually the absurdity of this whole charade will dawn on you. Each is playing a self-given role not determined by anyone else yet is assigned another role from outside by everyone in their life even as they do the same. Disappointment, judgment, conflict, and frustration then become inevitable. Honest and heartfelt communication based on the understanding of our own minds and the awareness of our self-justifying tendencies could bring much clarity into human relations if enough of us would make the effort to understand ourselves rather than defend ourselves.

The human mind is, in general, hunkered down in a constant position of attack and defense. Faced with a seemingly hostile and uncaring world, a world that appears outside of us and beyond our control, the common response is one of caution, careful planning, the search for security and the attempt to control the personal factors of life. This mindset carries over to our personal relations and interactions, becoming a kind of psychological configuration that dominates conscious and subconscious levels of mind, and through which we perceive and react to events and interactions with our fellow human beings. Fear and caution thus become the emotional backdrop to our lives though that may go unrecognized and usually does. Though we may desire and try to meet others from a position of openness and friendliness, the pervasive presence of unrecognized fear will always put limits on our feelings and behavior. A kind of emotional and psychological distance is maintained, and our human relations will tend to be confined to the superficial.

The role of fear in human life is not generally recognized. Each mind carries fear deep within and that fear takes many different forms: anger, hatred, sorrow, depression, anxiety etc. All emotions whose effect is to unbalance the mind's equilibrium, that weaken you, have their roots in fear. They are variations of fear, different forms of expression it takes in human life. It is essential to recognize the presence of fear in your mind, in your motivations, behavior, and attitudes. The influence of unacknowledged fear not only weakens us as individuals, but also weakens and distorts communication, making meaningful communication very difficult. Each of us is responsible for the state of our consciousness and our effect upon others, good or bad. The world situation as a whole is the result of the thoughts and behavior of each and every one of us. The action of fear must be replaced by the action of love, forgiveness, and compassion if the world situation is to change. We all share the responsibility for the present state of the earth and all must contribute to a solution.

It was a beautiful night, warm yet cooler after the overpowering heat of the day. A thunderstorm had brought much needed rain and the cool damp air smelled of moisture and aromatic plants. As darkness fell you could see the dark, low lying clouds to the south. They were moving very slowly, still filled with thunder and lightning. They were too far away to hear the thunder but the lightning was putting on a spectacular show. Every few seconds came another flash of light that lit up the sky. Most of the lightning could not be seen directly as it was hidden in the clouds, but several times a minute a lightning bolt was starkly visible as it traced its crooked path from sky to earth. Some split into two parts as they neared the earth like gigantic forks.

Do you ever wonder where lightning comes from, what

it is? I am sure the mind of man has an explanation and a definition for it that we may rest easy, thinking that through our labeling and analysis we have reached understanding. Does describing something, defining it, reducing it to concepts, lead to understanding? We have learned to manipulate some of the forces of nature, to use them, to direct them, but does this mean they are understood? Do we comprehend the thing in itself, what it is? The sheer beauty and awesome power of a bolt of lightning piercing time and space, connecting earth and sky, its simple and undeniable existence in itself, is not touched or captured by words or concepts, not even by mathematical formulas that describe its qualities, its workings. Lightning is not the word or the description. It is a part of existence itself, the great mystery that cannot be reduced to concepts nor understood by the reductionist functioning of the separative mind.

A small, muddy river, humble and simple, flows along one side of a shallow canyon. Its slow-moving water, laden with silt, brings life and color to the desert all around. A bright ribbon of green marks its course through the canyon and beyond. Many trees, cottonwoods, willows and others, provide leafy shelter along its banks and shade from the harsh glare of the desert sun. Under and among the trees grow many bushes and smaller plants; grasses cover the ground in many places, and here and there are patches of the large, white, bell-shaped flowers of the datura plant known as loco weed due to its effect on grazing animals that eat it.

Sometimes I think, as I look around at all the activity and movement that surround me and of which I am a part as I go about my business, that it seems as if we are all eating loco weed. Isolated in our little metal boxes on wheels, dashing about from place to place, constantly buying what we may or may not need, surrounded by the invitation, the temptation to buy this or do that, fascinated and absorbed by the possibilities of our modern society that continue to multiply far beyond the bounds of necessity; it is as if we are on a merry-go-round that never stops or slows down. In fact, the mad whirl that has become life keeps going faster and faster, not for any good reason but simply because it can. In order to attain more possessions and experiences, in order for the economy to keep growing which is considered a necessity by most, the pace of life must continue to get faster and faster. It's simple math: there are only twenty-four hours in a day; to accomplish more in the same interval of time you must go faster. Everywhere you can find some form of caffeine to fuel this frenzy of activity. And so we dash around from place to place, over caffeinated, overstimulated, frenzied, always on the move, always just one more purchase, one more stop then home to collapse in front of the television with a beer or glass of wine or perhaps some other drug of choice to help us recuperate from the day. Tomorrow is another day we think, or is it? Tomorrow's tasks may change; its demands on our time and energy may be different, but will its pace of activity, the constant traffic and our mindset, our state of consciousness, will that change?

A most fundamental truism of human life is that we are always doing exactly what we want to do even when we think otherwise. External factors, conditions and circumstances may seem to compel certain actions or behavior yet is it still a decision I make as an individual in the midst of my life's situations to do this or not do that. Am I forced to live this way; is it a free will choice? Do I like what my life has become? At some point, if you are so inclined, the question may arise: is this truly how I want to live, how I want to spend my days? To how many has this question occurred?

To simply follow along with the crowd, just reacting to situations and events, carried along in the great stream of modern life, adapting to what is presented me and accepting that this is just how life is: is this freedom? Is this happiness? Despite all our progress, it seems that a kind of desperation drives many, and the pace at which they live serves but to mask the problem and keep fear at bay.

Fear is the great crippler of the mind, interfering with clear thinking, and making appropriate decisions more difficult to achieve. All the while, fear holds the mind down, making real and lasting happiness impossible and driving motivation and behavior directly and indirectly. Love is and should be the proper source of our motivation and action. Where love is, there we find happiness also and freedom. Fear and love are incompatible; where one is, the other isn't. Life presents us with many choices as we go through each day. The possibilities for choice seem widely varied and almost unlimited, yet no matter the appearance there are always only two. You always choose based on love or fear. The surface of things, the level of appearances, the apparent details, are not where the fundamental choice is made. The details come and go, the content of our lives remains the same. Always we are thinking, feeling, and acting from a state of mind that is love or fear. Where we are in our mind is our gift to each other and to the world of which we are a part. Love joins with and heals, fear divides and destroys.

Mind is a house with many rooms
Divided in itself, unclear,
A house divided cannot stand.
Each room is made of many ideas.
Conflict within a room, conflict between rooms,
The war within has many fronts
But never a winner.
How can you defeat yourself without losing?
Cessation of conflict is the end of war,
Neither right nor wrong, just meaningless.

Thoughts arise in the mind
Their source true or false, real or unreal.

A constant parade across the screen of consciousness,
Dancing monkeys, restless, never at peace
Each holds the tail of the next.
Why do you follow them
And dance in a drunken parade
Going nowhere over and over?
Round and round without ceasing,
No destination or goal
Just noise and activity.

The Source of mind where all meaning lies
Cannot be found beneath your feet.
Thought cannot reach or hold it
Nor can desire reduce it to its grasp.
Only the Guide will take you there,
Only if you listen will you hear
His voice calling you, guiding you.
To listen is to ignore the din
Within the mind and choose silence.
Let Silence speak, listen to its Voice
Learn of that which words cannot touch.
You will become the Silence and
If any asks a question of you
You will laugh and the Silence
Will answer.

* * *

Sail across the great ocean
Of emptiness
Where the Titanic is constantly sinking.
Forget the lifeboats and jump
Into the sea, let the waves
Roll over you, sink beneath them

Into the depths where
Mind and body are not.
No I or me or you,
Become emptiness itself.
On the bottom of that sea
Lie the great ships every one.
Carry them on your back like stones,
Swim over them like the fish
Who never see the ocean
Though they are in it.
Stop breathing, making noise, struggling,
The ocean will hold you up.
Don't pretend you can't swim
When all you ever do is float
Among the waves.

* * *

The mighty storm approaches land.
All take refuge or flee the mighty winds.
Water surges everywhere, no place to hide,
Only the high ground is safe
The closest to heaven.
Rising above the lowlands, the ebb and flow
Of constant change buffet life.
Life is never without storms,
Each day brings potential disaster
Always it waits for your invitation.
Let the roof be blown off
Open your door that the waters may flow in.
When the house is swept away
No more troubles, nothing to worry about.
Free your possessions
That they may set you free.

The top of the mountain is bare,
Only the purity of snow
And the dignity of rock
Nothing more, and above
The endless sky.

What would you say if you were asked to name what is most important in your life? Is it your house, your car, other possessions or the bank account? Would your answer be husband or wife, lover, children, work or hobby? Could it be friends, activities, beliefs? Or some combination of things, activities, and relationships? Perhaps security, success, achievements, love or memories. As you consider this question, look deeply at your life, at what you value and what you desire, to what you aspire or hope to achieve. Look at the past, the goals you have had, what you have accomplished. Have they not changed over time, one goal taking the place of another; some goals reached and others perhaps discarded for whatever reasons? If you honestly consider your life and what has been valued and sought and protected, probably you will notice some changes, some shifting in what you had valued over time. Goals have seemingly changed, the forms of what you have sought or possessed and protected have also changed. All this change is the surface flow of your life, the details, conditions, and motivations that take different forms as you learn and grow as a human being over time. Underneath this surface movement, beyond form and variation, in the depth of being from where motivation arises, has your life really changed? Human life is a striving for something even if not recognized, an attempt to find happiness or peace or fulfillment, is it not? Are not all the things we would possess; our relationships, attainments, security, and our states of mind simply the conditions under which we believe we would be happy and at peace? Underneath our human strivings and goals, our many activities and constant restlessness, lies the desire, the need, to be happy, to leave fear behind and find love.

Happiness without love is impossible though many do not believe this. Those who seek to amass wealth and power can usually be successful only by depriving others in some way. To take from others is to take from yourself. This may not be readily apparent and usually is not but karmic law cannot be evaded; sooner or later you will reap the consequences of your actions. Because so many refuse to recognize the universal laws that govern us, human life is marked by war and genocide, greed and selfishness, the great wealth of the few and the poverty of the many. In the end, all are seeking the same thing but by many different means. If the means being used are not in accord with love but are a denial of it, the end result will not be happiness no matter how successful you may be outwardly.

To seek happiness among the things of this world is to not find it. True happiness is a state of mind, a part of your mind, being inherent in Consciousness Itself. Happiness need not be sought; rather seek out all that obstructs your awareness of it. All forms of fear, all judgment and condemnation of your fellow human beings, and all selfishness will banish happiness from awareness. Happiness will not leave your mind, being an aspect of it, but you will not experience it as long as you are busy denying love and welcoming fear in any of its forms. To attack love is to deny happiness; what you deny and attack, you will not experience.

The mind fluctuates between two emotions, two sources of motivation. Driven by fear it defends and attacks, or turns against itself and experiences sadness, depression or grief. Illuminated by Love, the mind gives, shares, joins with, and is helpful and kind to others. Love will never exclude for its nature is all inclusive; It will always give to all without exception. The highest expression of Love in this world is forgiveness. Like Love, forgiveness is given to all without regard to the offense, the hurt, the attack that is forgiven. Forgiveness is an action of mind in which all thought, all upset, all anger and judgment, are released and dissolved leaving only Love and a feeling of goodwill where once was a grievance. True forgiveness does not happen on the level of human mind where anger, hatred, and grievances are born. It comes from That which is highest in us, wiping the mind clean and releasing the heart from the burden it carries, leaving it free to love again.

When all you have ever wanted was Truth, the Truth, what do you do? Do you go on a pilgrimage to distant places, paying homage to those who have gone before? Do you sit alone at home in meditation from morning to night and drop out of society? Do you devote yourself to specific exercises and techniques of various kinds? Attend intensives and workshops, take classes on the Internet and read many books on various spiritual subjects? Or will you admit your total ignorance and ask for help from That Which is deep within you and in everything else as well and Which surrounds you at all times? In other words, are you willing to recognize you know nothing and surrender to a Power that is beyond your ego, beyond anything you have ever known, beyond your imagination? Are you willing to learn what cannot be grasped by the intellect or understood by the human mind, the ego mind? There is an unknown territory, a pathless land that all will reach in the end though they come from many directions and follow different sets of instructions. To discover this unknown territory is the purpose and goal of life, and all will come to realize this at some point in time.

Since everything is but an apparition, perfect in being what it is, having nothing to do with good or bad, acceptance or rejection, one may well burst out laughing.
Longchenpa

Chapter 5

Life

What is life? Is life a senseless journey through time and space ending in the dust from which the body arose? Or is life something more than that, of which the body's journey is only a part?

Nothing you see means anything
Yet what you see is what you get.
The body's eyes see only shadows
The many forms of emptiness.
Two eyes cannot see
What lies within and beyond form.
The eye must be single
To see the Light that shines
Within all things.
Form and shape, difference and size,
Color and movement, are veils
To distract the mind
And maintain its ignorance.

The mind's Source cannot be seen
It must be known.
Empty the mind of all you think and know,
Release the empty shell of desire.
Pleasure and pain are two sides
Of the same coin.
Throw away the counterfeit coins
They buy only misery and despair.
Learn to recognize where value lies
You value what is worthless,

Your treasure house is filled with sand.
Make your heart empty
That it may be filled again.
Throw away what you do not need.
Everything you carry with you is useless
As a sack of stones.
You cannot eat stones,
Find that bread which nourishes the soul.
Eat thereof and the fear of death
Will leave you forever.

What is most valuable in life is seldom recognized as such. The obvious, the tangible, draws our attention and our effort. What can be seen or perceived through the senses is easily believed in, is held to be real. What affects the body, i.e. the material world, easily convinces human consciousness of its reality. But this substantiality, this appearance of form and solidity is, to paraphrase Einstein, an optical delusion of human consciousness. The science of chemistry tells us that 99.9% of the area seemingly occupied by a material object is actually empty space due to the structure of the atoms of which it is comprised. Only a very small part of the occupied space is actually filled by the particles, by the material substance of the atom. Yet our senses tell us differently and we believe them implicitly though they are wrong. While it is true that we cannot avoid the effects we experience as material bodies, to jump to the conclusion that matter is the basis for all reality, for our lives, is premature. Many in our secular society hold this belief, not because it's a more rational conclusion than those underlying other belief systems, but because it's more obvious due to the evidence provided by the senses, misleading and questionable though it be. And there is, I might add, a cultural bias in our society towards materialism, due to our estrangement from nature and from any sense of being part of something greater, and the artificial lifestyle we have developed not to mention the very self-centered and egocentric emphasis on individual freedom which implies a presupposed completeness and sufficiency of each separate person. There is not much room in such a mindset for the simplest and most obvious question posed to us by the very fact of our conscious existence. What am I and what is the purpose and meaning of my life?

When I look at what is going on around me in society at large: the high rate of suicide, the high rate of drug and alcohol addiction among other self-destructive behaviors, our isolation from each other and the divisiveness that permeates society, all the very popular entertainment based on horror, murder, graphic violence, and magical fantasies, and the unceasing pursuit of more pleasure, more stimulation and more toys, more escapes, that is very common among young and old alike. When I observe and ponder what I see all around me, it does not look like a civilization full of happy campers despite the unparalleled level of affluence and comfort that prevails among a large segment of the population. I can't help but think that the modern definition of what a human being is, and the lack of purpose to life that is at least implied in this view, has something to do with our increasing dysfunction and obvious unhappiness. Our societal experts, the intellectuals, academics etc. through our educational institutions and the various media present this reductionist image of what you are as if it were proven fact, which it isn't, and many seem to have swallowed this poison pill without really even thinking the matter over.

I remember how for a time as a young man I accepted this view uncritically until my experience of life called it into question. When I began to truly examine the issue, it did not stand up to the light of honest inquiry and serious reason. The incompleteness of the materialistic view, its biases and unexamined, unproven a priori assumptions became obvious. There are those who regard this "modern view" of what we human beings are and the implied fundamental lack of purpose in our existence, not to mention its propagation and presentation to us as fact, as a betrayal of humanity, of the human spirit. You can decide for yourself but I urge you to think earnestly about it, to examine the matter with an open mind. In any case, it's wise to remember that human life is based on a sense of meaning that lies beyond our biological imperatives. Eating, sleeping, and having sex are not bad things, being part of our lives, but there is something within most of us that recognizes we are more than just beasts and our life is about more than fulfilling desires and satisfying biological urges.

What is it that makes the human race the human race? What is most essentially human about us and our lives? Perhaps we can say that our sense of a purpose beyond the mundane details of life, a purpose we all share, a sense of meaning that is available to all, is certainly one of the essentials that make us human and this has historically been present to some degree or another in virtually all human societies from the most primitive up to the present day. This recognition, this feeling or intuition, is not simply a cultural artifact to be discarded like many others have been over the course of our history. The sense of purpose and meaning has been universally present during the march of human progress and development though its expressions can be culturally determined at any given time by any given culture. The modern belief system about the nature of reality called materialism is also a culturally determined artifact of our civilization; it is not the final and ultimate view of the nature of reality objectively arrived at, as our modern mythology claims, but simply a new set of biases that are for the most part unexamined.

Religion has its starting point as the direct experience of the deeper, also called transcendent, dimensions of being and consciousness that lie beyond the limited, everyday state of mind grounded in physical experience and the mental and emotional responses to it. The origin of religion is thus the transcendental. What follows afterwards, however, is often problematic. Attempts to organize what has been discovered, the creation of an institution to present and perpetuate it, brings the human ego into the process. Ambition, control issues, power trips, financial considerations etc. then follow. Human beings, being human and thus less than perfect and capable of self-serving behavior and error, tend to muddy the waters and reduce the original teaching to something other than what it was, at least in the practice of it. Be that as it may, religion can generally exert a positive effect on society and individuals as long as its excesses, like the excesses of any other human institutions, can be tempered or controlled by civil law and social custom.

The desert never fails to amaze me with its starkly bare veneer of sand and rock and yet the wide variety of life forms that inhabit it. Mesquite trees, with their sharp thorns to protect their branches, nonetheless provide shade and shelter for all. Their pods provide food for other desert creatures as well as for the native people who lived here in the past. Prickly pear cacti provide an edible fruit that can be harvested if you know how to remove the fruit from the plant. Everything that lives in the desert, plant or animal, is strong and resilient. The plants are often prickly and tough, many of the animals bite or sting, some with very painful even lethal effect. Many animals lay low during the day, taking shelter under rocks, in holes or in the shade that plants provide. Once the sun goes down the desert comes alive as all begin the never-ending quest for food. From the smallest to the largest, from wolf spider and scorpion to coyote, deer, and javelina, all must eat as must human beings.

In the modern era, we have our food supply well organized. Most of us do not spend hours a day growing our food or searching for it. Our day is filled by other necessities, mainly the need to work which brings us what we need in the form of money to purchase food, shelter, clothing, often a car. Like the desert creatures, the lives of many of us are also dominated by the activity that provides us with the means to survive.

As human beings, many of us also live in a desert, a kind of inner wasteland that we try to fill with activities, with possessions and accomplishments. We seek ourselves in relationships where we share love, or at least we try. Can you find yourself in a relationship with something or someone outside of you? Can love be found without or must you turn within to find it in yourself before you can give it, before you can share it? Too often our relationships with others arise from a sense of insufficiency, of unworthiness, and they suffer as a result.

When you tell someone, "I love you," what does that mean really? Do we love them for what they give us, for how they make us feel? Do we love them for themselves, and if they disappoint us by not fulfilling our demands or expectations, do we still love them? Or does "love" suddenly change to anger or even hate? Too often human love is based on mutual dependence, on compromise and pleasing each other, on passing fancies such as sexual attraction or romantic fantasies. Are these things a suitable basis from which love can grow into a mutual give and take that does not arise from need? The basis of real love, a lasting love, is selflessness not selfishness, and a freedom and a giving that does not demand recompense but recognizes that the interests of one are the same as the interests of the other. Mature love rests on respect for each other and the refusal to impose demands which is based on recognition of the necessity of freedom. Where love is, there is freedom also. Love without freedom is not worthy of the name.

Freedom is not the absence of restraint; it is not license to do what you please. Freedom has nothing intrinsic to do with the body's activities, with its limitations, with our endless restlessness.

Is freedom seen from without

Or known from within?
Bodies are not free
Gravity holds them to earth.
Buffeted by wind, drenched by rain
Swept away in an instant
By rising waters.
Does an inert object
Floating on the rising tide
Proclaim its freedom
Even as it is carried away?
Does a body tell death
When it comes to call,
"Go away, you cannot touch me
I am free."
All bodies return to dust, to ashes.
Death cannot touch freedom.

Is freedom a state of nothing left to lose?
Where attachment is and fear of loss
Freedom will not be found.
The absence of fear, no dependence,
No attachment to things or conditions,
Is the beginning of freedom.
A flower grows where it is planted.
No question of freedom or bondage,
Just growing, flowering
Fulfilling the purpose of its existence.
Without fear, without thinking
Just being what it is
The inherent simplicity of life.

How difficult for the human being,
Many choices, decisions, responsibilities
Continuously demand attention.

Everything so important though it leads nowhere.
Complexity obscures, complications obstruct
The unnecessary appears as necessity
Mind becomes cloudy, confused
Spins around in circles of its own making.
All circles have an exit
If you will only look.
Help waits beyond the circle,
Make an opening in your mind
And It will visit you.
Treat It as an honored guest.
It will tear down the walls of your house,
The walls that imprison you,
Freedom is not seen in darkness.
Tear off the roof, break down the doors
Welcome the Light that shines so brightly.
You cannot hide behind walls
And find the freedom that awaits.
The eagle that never leaves the ground
Will never know the vastness of the sky.

Sometimes I envy the white clouds as they float lazily across the sky; soft, billowy, fantastic shapes of the purest white. The late afternoon sun lights them up, bringing out shape and shadow. As the sun sinks beneath the horizon, the sky becomes a deeper blue and the white clouds glow with a golden light. Sometimes a soft pink joins the yellow and golden hues that fill the western sky, and it seems, for just a moment, that a little bit of heaven's beauty has come to earth.

There is beauty all around us each and every day if we will only look. The sky above, the earth below, all the life that surrounds us with its sounds, its songs, its continuous movement, is a constant dance of creation carrying the world along like a boat floating on a great river. The river itself is unstoppable. Each moment is different from the one before and the one that follows yet all are linked together as one. The play of personalities goes on and on as each mind takes on the characteristics determined by its past experience and karma. Life presents its lessons over and over to each of us in many different forms. Sooner or later each lesson is learned then it's on to the next one. Learning never stops as life itself is learning. Though the lessons seem to be many, there are really only two that are presented again and again in an endless variety of seeming choices in the midst of constantly changing conditions and circumstances. Likewise, the range of choices is limited although they seem to appear in many different guises. Always only two, the inner content of every choice you are called upon to make. The purpose of variety and complexity is to mask the simplicity of what is to be learned. The mind, so long lost and absorbed in that which has no meaning, has lost the directness of simplicity. Its ability to recognize and accept the essentials is severely limited by the conceptual overlay and mental patterning through which it attempts to perceive and understand.

You are a living part of a great and mysterious expression and movement that is constantly changing, growing, dying, being born. A riot of color, activity, shapes and sizes, of creativity and chaos, surrounds, contains, and pervades our lives. Despite the human mind's attempt to separate itself from all this, the sense of and belief in our separate and separative existence is an illusion. In our modern era, it must be admitted, we have constructed a very powerful and convincing illusion of separateness and control over nature due to our inventiveness in general and science in particular. Life for many has been somewhat relieved of much of the discomfort and physical suffering that characterized our past and this is a good thing. Unfortunately, however, everything invented by the human ego eventually turns out to be a double-edged sword that can cut both ways, good and bad. The belief in our ability and right to control nature and bend her to our will has resulted in much damage to the natural world and to the earth herself; damage that cannot easily be undone. This has introduced new hazards into our existence such as pollution with its set of problems, and poisons that end up in our bodies affecting our health, even in life-threatening ways.

Look honestly at what we are doing as a civilization and it is difficult to deny that we are apparently engaged in a campaign to destroy the very earth beneath our feet, the earth that is our home, that provides us with food, shelter, and the raw materials for our technology. No matter how the necessities of life are modified and their production controlled by modern methods and technology, they still come to us from nature herself, from the living and nonliving systems of Mother Earth. No one has yet invented a long-term substitute for food, for the necessity to eat. There is no app for that. The digital "revolution" has not yet come up with a substitute for eating. Artificial intelligence can do some of our thinking and some of our physical tasks, but it cannot live our life for us. Only we can do that. Life itself is not mechanical; it is imperfect and at times destructive and chaotic. Yet, we are a part of it and that will not change. No matter how we try to control nature and reduce her offerings to conform to our mania for consumption and possessions, we are still a part of nature and subject to her conditions in many different ways. The appearance of great control over the natural world is not what it seems. Life cannot be reduced to a facsimile of a theme park.

What is it to live truly?
What makes life worth living?
The pain and suffering of our fellows
Impacts us each and every one.
None live in isolation
All belong to the Whole.
The Whole that is humanity

The Whole that is life itself.
The Whole that is love and compassion
The Whole that is the Earth.
Yet isolation rules and separation
Seems to be the condition of life.
Nothing is what it seems
In a world of mirrors and shadows.

The body is an image
Appearing in the mirror of time and space,
A shadow thrown against a wall
That rises up before us.
Physicality, seemingly solid, impenetrable
Devoid of real substance
Does it really exist?
Beyond perception is there anything
That exists beyond question?
Questions without answers
And answers to meaningless questions
Are equally meaningless, valueless.
To whom do questions arise and for what reasons?
Reasons there are many
As many as questions.
Can you absorb a question
Let it become part of you
Does it then require an answer?

Is Truth a question to be asked
Or a fact that requires discovery?
Thinking that leads only to more questions
Is useless, a play of words
To keep the mind so busy
It cannot recognize its origin.
Of what use is it

To cover life with concepts
And evade the meaning it would
Reveal to you if you would listen?
Being is its own answer
To the question you do not ask.
The only one that is its own answer.
Beyond thinking, questions and answers
Is the certainty of Truth.
Nothing else.

* * *

You who walk the earth with heavy steps
Listen to your footfalls
Echoing down the halls of time.
Is there a sound you do not hear
In the air all around?
A happy song in praise of life
A blessing given to all.
How many really listen
To the songs waiting to be written?
No one can write your song but you.
Listen and you will hear it.
Its melody you know
You brought it with you
When you came.
Now write the words that
Cannot be heard or spoken.
Being has no words or images,
Creativity unfolding beyond thought or feeling
Just vastness like the ocean
Unconcerned with what floats
On its surface.

Can we consider the question of how we know what we know? Start at the beginning with the only thing you know for sure. You know that you are, that you exist. How do you know this? You are most fundamentally self-aware, i.e. you are aware and you are aware that you are aware. There is also in that a sense of conscious being, a sense that you have or are being or a being, an entity or some thing that is conscious of being conscious. Now, in the state of being that you find yourself in in this world, you are also aware in a fundamental way that you perceive, you sense objects and sounds all around you. This includes the body which you experience to be a location in space vis-á-vis other objects, and that is experienced as the means or thing through which you experience perception. You could say that from this very fundamental awareness of perception and the body (the body is also an object of perception) arises the first fundamental assumption of your existence: the body is what I am, i.e. the body is my being or identity, or at the very least, a basic and very important part of it. Other basic assumptions then also arise. As the thinking process appears in the mind, in awareness, and as through awareness you are conscious of thoughts through a kind of inner perception, another assumption arises. These thoughts of which I am aware are present in my awareness in a kind of inner sensing as opposed to my perceptions of what happens outside the space the body occupies. They thus seem to belong to me or are part of me like the body so they must be my thoughts. The sense of being the thinker of thoughts joins the sense of being a body and also becomes a part of my identity. Now, as a result of the assumptions that I am this body and I am the owner or thinker of thoughts, a sense of fundamental identity begins to be established in my mind. It can best be described as a belief or sense that I am an entity, a person who is aware of being a body, a body which is perceived by mind as different from mind, as of another order of existence. And I also seem to be a mind which is somehow in this body despite being of a different nature and, as mind, I am a thinker of thoughts as well as a perceiver of things, be they objects apparently outside of my location such as trees, fences, clouds etc., or things apparently arising in my consciousness and perceived inwardly which I may call thoughts, feelings, emotions, sensations etc. The sort of melding of body and mind in certain of my perceptions, such as bodily sensations like pain which are experienced as within me, blurs distinctions between body and mind and seems to suggest an identity that can best be described as a body/mind.

A kind of dichotomy of body and mind as separate aspects or parts of the human being was for a long time a part of human thinking. In the modern era, under the influence of the belief in materialism, and as a result of scientific research into the brain which has shown an association between brain activity, thinking, and certain emotional states, the belief or assumption has arisen that consciousness itself as well as its activities is nothing more than the brain. Ergo, you are nothing more than a "meat machine," a composition of flesh and its activity which is somehow self-aware and conscious of a world that is both within and without. It has not been proven that consciousness arises only from brain activity, though in the modern reductionist thought system that has become popular, this belief is accepted as if it were as fact rather than fantasy. In fact, there is much "anecdotal experience," the individual life experiences of untold numbers of people throughout our history and right up to the present day, that strongly suggests the opposite: the mind or consciousness is beyond the brain, beyond physicality as we know it and is not limited to it. We could say that awareness, that consciousness is its own dimension, that it has existence in and of itself. Consciousness does not arise simply as a byproduct of physical processes though it may also function through them in a kind of interface with physical bodies, the brain, and the nervous system. The identification of consciousness with the body, at least in a reductive sense, is nothing more than an assumption, a kind of wishful thinking; it is not a fact.

Our lives as living, feeling, thinking, experiencing beings are a direct experiencing of the "inner" and "outer" dimensions of our existence. Virtually all of our day to day experience of whatever kind is individual even if it takes place in tandem with others. Thus much or most of our life experiences can be described as anecdotal. This does not make them invalid, unreal, or untrue. It does not make the discoveries and experiences of our lives not valuable in relation to what is true, what is truth or reality.

Mind as such, as awareness
Is free and unconditioned.
The body appears in mind
As an image of perception
Unnecessary, yet there nonetheless.
Everything is an apparition
Appearing in mind,
Fulfilling itself as what it is
Having nothing to do with thinking,
With judgments of good or bad.
No reason behind appearance
No reason behind non-appearance
Just here, just there, yet nowhere.

What would you say
If I told you
You are just a figment
Of your own imagination?
Examine the assumptions you have made
Such as:
I am a self, a person
I am a body in time/space.
The body lives so I live
The body dies so I die.

How do you know
Any of this is true?
Cloudy and confused
Mind ceases to know itself.

The ignorance of Truth
Arises from assumptions.
Assumptions are based on thinking,
Thinking arises from the past
Thought is always the past.
You live only in the freshness
Of the present.
Thought is the map, you are the territory.

What is it to experience anything
If you don't know your own Being?
Experience is a projection
Outside of you but part of your mind.
While you do not believe this
You will not know your own Self.
Like images appearing in a mirror
The world surrounds you,
Ephemeral forms and shapes
Changing all the time.
Essence is unchanging, unaffected
By the play of projection.
Return to essence.

* * *

The sun rises just for you.
Why else would it rise?
Only madness thinks otherwise.
Walk through the desert thornbush

Pay no attention to the wounds.
Let them bleed like roses,
The scent of thorns is sweet
If you are wounded by the rose.
Beauty and innocence need no protection
Thorns are just for show.
Pay no attention, they will fade away
Blood need not be spilled.

Give away all you have
And a stranger will come knocking.
Don't hide behind the door
Open it, let him in.
"There is no room for me
At the inn," he will say.
Invite him in, give him
The remains of your house.
You don't need it anymore.
A house empty of possessions
Will fall down. Its only use
Was to hold what you
Have given it.

Give everything away, then give away
Your head full of ideas.
They bring you nothing, just more ideas
And confusion to dull the mind.
A dull knife cannot cut through
The rind which hides the fruit within.
The Essence is like the kernel of a precious fruit
Hidden by the thick skin without.
It cannot be revealed unless
The mind is like a gleaming blade
Reflecting the sunlight as it cuts

To the core, to the Sun within.
That Sun's rays will blind you
Till all shadows disappear
Leaving you to stand naked
In pure radiance.

Just as the sun rises each morning in the East because that is its function, to rise in the East and set in the West and illuminate everything in between, you also have a function, a task assigned you to fulfill. Like the sun, your task in this world begins with your birth in the East which brings joy to your parents and to the earth. All of life rejoices that another light has come from beyond our range of sight to walk the earth and shine through the darkness. Another beacon is set high on a hill for all of us to join with, that we may share our light with each other and lighten the load each carries. We are not meant to crawl about the surface of the earth like pitiful creatures looking only for food and a little pleasure, and hiding each in his/her own hole where there is no room for life to grow, to flourish and blossom. Security is not found by burrowing into the earth, by hiding behind a collection of possessions worth no more than a pile of dung. Safety is not assured by defenses and isolation, by attacking ourselves and others.

The way of the world is a kind of sadness, fueled by fear, selfishness, and the denial of Love. I am not speaking here of "romantic love," which is a kind of emotional delusion though it may include elements of selflessness that reflect Love as it truly is. The Love of which I am speaking is a universal power, a force; Love is the source of all creation and is its motivating force. No greater power exists. This has been expressed by religion as "God is Love." What is perhaps not so simply and clearly expressed in religious teachings is that you are Love. Each of us in this world, though appearing as separate beings, are joined in the Oneness that is Love. Love is a part of our Essence, That of which we are an apparent expression in this world of time and space and materiality.

We are "born" into the world, we come into the world with a purpose. This is spoken of in the Wisdom Traditions of humanity as well as the Religious Traditions. Our purpose can generally be described as one in which we are to learn the truth of what we are and become that in our lives, become that in our minds and hearts. The truth of what we are, each and every one, includes Love. Our purpose can thus be expressed as the goal of becoming consciously aware of the Love that is our core, and living from that as that in our everyday life. "Faith without works is dead," as stated in the New Testament of the Bible, is a thought that can also be applied to Love. Love is active, generous, including all, giving to all, forgiving, helpful, humble and much, much more. To live from Love, as Love, is to be Its expression in this world. To say I love you is good; to act from Love is better. Living in a state of being Love, not simply having mental ideas about Love, is to be an expression of Love in thought, word and deed; to be a center of Love shining forth in a world which denies It.

There's too much to do to speak about.
Words are so useless though helpful.
Let them go, you fool.
I am speaking to myself.
You can listen if you wish
But you won't learn anything from me.
I have nothing to say yet
Words keep spilling from my mouth
And bounce along the ground
Like marbles with no place to go.
My pen keeps writing words on paper.
It doesn't need me.
I know nothing and that
Is better than knowing something.

The words that spill from my mind
Don't belong to me the way
This chair belongs to me.
They come from somewhere else,
A knowing that belongs to all.
I happened to come by like a taxi
And the words jumped in so I
Delivered them to their destination.
Now you must, if you wish
Ferry them to their new home
In someone's heart. I will see
You there in the heart where
All lovers live. It doesn't matter
What you love, the wrapping or sound
Of it covers the only One Who
Can be loved, the One Who made
Love what It is.

Can you love another without loving yourself? Is it possible to give love without having it? To love is to give; you cannot give what you do not have. To love is to give everything, all of yourself. This is an action of mind and heart that bypasses the fixation on bodies, on things, though that love may help those who live as bodies. Love can fill the world with hope and kindness; doors will open and smiles may break out on a thousand faces. Always we can choose to open the door and smile, or hide behind it and refuse to love and be loved. Like everything in this life, love is a choice that can be made. In the choosing of anything it is strengthened in your mind. Choose love again and again, and you will become one of those whose smile is an invitation to Eternity.

I am nothing, just an image
Appearing on a stage, a clown

Without makeup and a name.
The rain falling from heaven
Falls on the roof
Then through a drain pipe
It reaches the earth.
Some of us are like drain pipes.
The manna which falls from above
Pours through us to reach the earth
Where it nourishes the flowers.

* * *

Do not let the lessons Love teaches
Pass you by on the road.
The road leads nowhere if you leave Love behind.
There is a golden city filled with precious stones
At the end of all roads.
It may take a long time to get there
And the journey may be interrupted many times.
Do not let death control your destiny.
Death wears the mask of pleasure and pain
Of fear and conflict, never the smile of Love.
A great Love shines away fear.
In its eyes, death loses its power
To separate and control.
Death is a drunken clown dancing in a graveyard.
Those who die before they die
Need no tombstone to mark their place.
The grave cannot hold them.
In their silence, time and space are no more
And Love's smile covers all.

* * *

All there is to say
Has already been said so many times.
Why can't we listen to those
Who have gone before and left
Their wisdom behind to guide us?
Humanity has been given the wise ones
Who speak for us all
Who learned what we must learn
And lived the way we must live.
Not just their words but their lives
Were a teaching for us all.
In many languages, through many eras
Guidelines were given, principles revealed
Taking different forms as did
The messengers who brought them.
Using various words and symbols
Again and again repeated, renewed.
What else is there to say but this?
Truth is One, though clothed
In many different forms
Described in many different ways.
Many paths can be taken
To reach the One, only One.
Use the teaching that inspires you,
The one to which you were led.
Surrender the knowledge you think
You have, it is only the past.
Holding onto the past is like
Reading last week's newspaper
And imagining that it is now.
Today, here and now, is where
You will find your life.
You don't live yesterday or tomorrow.
Life is the present unfolding in you

Around you as you.
The river will carry you along whether
You are floating face up looking
At the sky or face down
Examining the muddy bottom.
The river doesn't care what you do
It holds you up anyway.
Your choice to sink or swim with the current.
Be a stone, you will sink to the bottom
The mud will be your home.
Be a swan and paddle steadily
Towards the river's end.
When you reach the ocean
You will spread your great white wings and fly
And freedom will be your home.

All things purposeless and temporary will pass away
leaving only Truth in the end.
From the Christ Mind

Chapter 6

Awareness and Intelligence

Thinking is most fundamentally a movement in awareness, a more or less constant stream of thoughts, images, impulses, and feelings that appear in conscious awareness without cessation during waking hours. Thinking is also that particular process of thought that is directed towards a particular goal or used to bring about clarity and understanding in relation to some thing or idea. In that case, there seems to be an agent, a "thinker" who takes charge of the otherwise automatic movement of mind and directs and controls it to reach a desired end. A third kind of thinking is when the seemingly automatic and somewhat random process of the movement of thought seems to limit itself to focus on a particular issue or situation in the mind of the thinker, a kind of active obsessing without the mind being directed to do so as is the case with consciously directed thought. In this type of thinking, an emotional concern or investment most often appears to be the source or motivation for the focus. There is another type of thinking that arises from intuition – i.e. we know but we do not know how we know and... Closely related to intuition is the process we call inspiration as found in art, science, inventions or new solutions to problems. This is a specific movement of thought that spontaneously arises in awareness and carries within it information that was not previously known or imagined. And finally there is the process of active imagination.

Virtually all thinking can be described by these categories. The most fundamental process of thinking is, in its most basic sense, constant, automatic, and marked by a certain randomness. The other types of thinking impose a focus or direction or limitation temporarily on the constant movement of thought. As soon as that focus is broken, however, thought returns to its continuous flow across the screen of conscious awareness, coming from we know not where and disappearing likewise from our inner perception.

What is the source or meaning of all this activity? The famous maxim of Descartes, "I think, therefore I am," implies that thought is the proof or the measure of existence. Actually it is more accurate to say that because I am aware of my thinking, I exist. There cannot be thought without the awareness of it. Awareness itself, whether of inner objects such as thoughts or outer objects of perception such as trees, houses, etc., is the most fundamental level or property or aspect of mind. Therefore Descartes' maxim is more accurately expressed as: I am aware I am thinking, therefore I am. I am aware of my thoughts, therefore I am.

What is the role of belief and association in thinking? Some beliefs are long forgotten and lost to conscious awareness but exert an influence on thinking nonetheless because they still live in the mind. Others can be consciously recalled yet we are not consciously aware of them most of the time even though they affect our thinking and responses to the world around us. To be able to connect our beliefs, especially our core beliefs to our thought processes, our value judgments, and our reactions to our life experiences are very important. Without this awareness, our mind reacts automatically and repetitively in habitual ways that are severely limiting and deadening to life itself.

Whatever is the cost of attaining what we truly value, we will pay it, for we believe that what is thereby attained is worth more than what we must pay for it. The goal is always seen as exceeding in value the means by which it is attained. Human life always proceeds on the basis of what is valued and the activity necessary to achieve it and maintain its possession. Values themselves are taught, handed down from one generation to the next, or they are learned in the process of living through the example of others we respect and admire. Always they come to us secondhand, used by others, and through that use and acceptance, their validity established. Values include those that have been long established as the basis for our moral and ethical decisions, many of which could be regarded as universal and always necessary for human life, and those whose existence and acceptance is more a matter of cultural and temporal factors that can and do change. And there are those values that have to do with our self-concept, how we live our lives, how we treat others, and how we pursue our own self-interest.

It is here that the modern value paradigm has done the most damage to the human spirit and human life in general. Wherever there is the operation of a kind of reductionism, an effort to reduce something to simpler and simpler definitions, the thing in question is denied or deprived of some of its attributes and possibilities until it is, at worst, reduced to a caricature of itself and deprived of much of its potential functioning. Such is the valuation placed on the modern human being by the reductionist "explanation" of what is a human being and its origin.

Within the context of materialist thought, the paradigm of materialism, human beings are seen as little more than "smart monkeys with clothes on," a kind of latter day primate with tennis shoes and a computer, the latest and arguably most intelligent great ape to walk the earth. And, to add insult to injury, humanity, like all of life, is simply the product of a blind, random, accidental, purposeless and meaningless process that has somehow, for no good reason, produced an incredibly broad and varied spectrum of life forms that nevertheless, certainly in the most advanced forms, exhibit consistent purpose and a sense of meaning.

This view of what a human being is, is not only degrading, but is a betrayal of humanity itself. It simply throws out of the picture or denies significant and consistent parts of human experience throughout history, insisting that such experience is illusory thus invalidating it. This is done on the basis of no proof, evidence, or even a good faith attempt to study human experience in a fair, open-minded and truly scientific manner.

In the face of such a narrow, arrogant, and close-minded view of what you are, you are left with the choice so well expressed by Groucho Marx many years ago. "Who are you gonna believe, me or your own eyes?" The obviously sane response would seem to be to seriously consider and respect the validity of your own experience and that of others whom you respect. It is a sad fact, however, that the tendency of the mind to be conditioned according to upbringing and education not to mention the constant influence of the media, leads to a kind of constantly reinforced consensus view of human reality and reality altogether that is in nature reductionist.

The mind functions always in the most basic sense from and as an expression of a fundamental belief system about what it is and what the reality is in which it apparently finds itself. This cannot be too strongly emphasized. Our values and understanding are strongly influenced in their development or determined by our most fundamental beliefs about ourselves and our relationship to the world around us. A self-image based on a severely reduced idea of what we truly are and what our function should be, a view that denies much of historical experience and learning not to mention some or much of our potential experience, has a powerfully weakening effect on the human spirit. The modern human is thus left with no relationship to the great sweep of human thought and experience throughout history. Thus you are left with no relationship to real purpose and meaning, and are saddled with the identity of a thinking, tool-using animal whose purpose is to eat, drink, have sex, procreate, pursue various forms of stimulation and pleasure, and pursue goals that promise temporary security physically, mentally, and emotionally, while never questioning why you live or how or to what purpose beyond immediate gratification. And you are defined in a most practical and continuous way as nothing more than a consumer of goods and services and your purpose is to amass as much in the way of possessions and material wealth as possible. Such a life, distracting and temporarily gratifying as it may be, is but the most superficial dimension of existence, barely above the animal level, and lacks the depth and meaning that would bring true peace and fulfillment.

Whatever you do, do it with full attention and put your whole heart into it. What does it mean to put your entire heart into a task? Surely it is to bring love and full attention to your undertaking, to bring passion, not the passion of Eros but the passion that is a full affirmation of the present and the importance of whatever you are doing. It matters not the significance of the task in worldly terms or in the eyes of others. Simply by virtue of the fact you are led by compulsion, necessity, or attraction to engage in a particular action makes it important and deserving of your full participation.

Life must be lived fully, with the full engagement of all faculties, or it becomes but a pale shadow of itself, scarcely worth the time and effort. Authentic engagement with all that surrounds you, full participation in the beauty, wonder, and mystery of existence is a necessity if you are to make the most of what you are and what you have been given.

Such a life requires discipline, focus, and real interest. Not the harsh discipline you force upon yourself according to some idea, ideal, or goal, but the natural inclination that arises from the recognition of what is truly valuable and worthy of effort. Serious intent, fortified by determination and consistently expressed through perseverance, gives rise to a natural discipline which, though it may still involve some struggle as resistance may arise, lacks the harshness and violence that characterize the discipline directed at a lesser goal. An undisciplined mind can do nothing but act out its impulses, biases, and compulsions in varying degrees. We see this in the realm of addiction to alcohol, drugs or certain behavior. The self-destructiveness that results is readily apparent and deeply saddening.

It is a fact of human life that every human being needs meaning or purpose, a central focus around which life is structured, a basis from which to live. This can take many different forms, but all forms it may take must be meaningful or fulfilling in some basic sense to the individual life. Family, job or profession, hobby, human relationships, the pursuit of goals or attainments: these are some of the more common ways in which we as human beings attempt to give life purpose and meaning.

When through choice or disinclination an individual lacks anything to give their life direction and purpose in a positive sense, the void at the center of their life will be filled in by addictive, escapist, and self-destructive behavior. This is inevitable, for the deep emptiness that lies beneath the surface of consciousness must be filled whether in a positive or a negative sense; it cannot be otherwise. Life faced with this voidness at its core will rush to destruction unless some distraction is chosen to fill or avoid the emptiness.

The answer to the question of the transcendent is also the answer to the meaning and purpose of life. This answer informs, shapes, and influences our life whether the answer be affirmative or negative. This question can only and ultimately be answered by the direct experience that is only available to the individual mind.

It is impossible logically, using words and concepts, reason and arguments, to answer this question definitively, although a very good case can be made for the affirmative answer. Likewise, using the empirical approach of everyday experience and the empiricism of science, a definitive answer cannot be reached that dispels all doubt one way or the other. To those who have the very broad range of experience that extends beyond the parameters of the merely physical, the authenticity of direct experience is certain proof of the existence of the Transcendental. This is a solution only an individual can find directly. Indirect proof will never be convincing.

The issue simply stated: The answer to the true nature of Reality and thus the true nature of the human being, of human existence, can only be found on the level of individual mind. Every individual must answer this question sooner or later until the correct answer is found through experience. To base your answer on experience, which is the empirical approach also used by science, is ultimately the only way to reach certainty. Experience brings conviction. However, what is very important here is the recognition that you must not stop on the level of the obvious physical and perceptual experience and base your belief on this unstable and incomplete foundation, but must press on and honestly discover that wider spectrum of experience that lies beyond space/time limitations and the subject/object duality.

The One who made us has given us everything we have or need. The Light in your eyes is His Gift. The mind you use to think with is His Mind. The Love you feel within your heart is His Love. His Grace is ever flowing to you if you would but receive it. By Grace we live though not often are we aware of It. By Grace we are released into the Eternal Life we share with God and all living things. All of Creation lifts its voice in praise of the Creator; we must join this song if we would know Him and recognize His Grace in our lives. Our appreciation will become gratitude, and gratitude belongs to Love. God knows us through Love; through His Love we come to know Him and enter into communion with Him and all things.

Is Love many or is Love One?
Can we love many or only the One?
To love God is to love your neighbor.
Your neighbor lives in God
As do you. He is a whole
Part of God as are you.

To not love your neighbor
Is not to love a part of God.
How can that be?
Thou shalt love thy neighbor
As thyself for he is thyself.
As One, you are joined in God.
Never will this change.
Whoever you know, see, hear, remember
Or think about is your neighbor.
To be safe, love everybody.
Just let the Love hidden
In your heart out of its cage.
Leave the cage door open
Love will do the rest.
It will carry you along
Like a mighty wave that crashes
Onto the shore of the Great Sea.

See the black robed figures,
The apostles of fear as they carry
Bodies to the fire.
All bodies will be consumed
By fire, decay. They will crumble
Into dust but Love will not die.
Love is eternally new, born again
And again in the hearts of those
Who welcome It.
Love conquers all.
Even death must yield its seeming victory
To Love's triumphant smile.

Can anything good ever come from fear, from giving in to fear?
Can a state of mind that is fearful ever accomplish anything? No
matter the outward appearances or circumstances, does reacting

to them with fear benefit you at all? Does fear help you respond in an appropriate manner to the demands of the moment? I am not referring to the fear that may be appropriate to physical circumstances such as being perched on the edge of a great, high cliff. I am referring to the psychological fear that haunts the minds of humanity, the fear that is learned or unconscious; this habitual and automatic fear takes the form of a background anxiety that may always be with you, or it may take the form of the often irrational and defensive reactions in certain situations where we may react in a manner that is way out of proportion to the perceived threat, even to the point of projecting threat where there is none.

Much of humanity is haunted by unexamined fear that often lies at the root of our motivations and behavior. It is unfortunately true that the conscious experience of fear, of fearful states, is probably the most uncomfortable experience that we may have as human beings. As a result, most people will avoid possible fear-provoking situations at all costs. In other words, we are literally afraid of fear. This fear of feeling fear makes it extremely difficult to rationally approach the fear in your mind, to learn to recognize it and take the necessary steps to release it, to clear it from your consciousness.

Very commonly in human life we follow a pattern of living that attempts to keep fear away, though we cannot keep away what so deeply penetrates our minds indefinitely. This attitude itself, this default on the issue of knowing and understanding our own minds, leads to a life marked by unconscious behavior, perhaps even by a consistent tendency to escape from the feelings that life's changes can arouse, and to consistent habits of suppression and avoidance.

Freedom and real self-fulfillment are not found by avoidance of life's situations and conditions. You will not find freedom by running from or suppressing fear but by facing it, understanding it, and rejecting its dominance, its effect on you. Freedom cannot become the condition in which you live while you are committed to the continuation in your mind of that which limits and imprisons you. The bars and walls that hold your mind a prisoner to fear will not disappear unless you take responsibility for them and act to tear them down. When you decide to do so, the help you need will be given you.

The crickets continue their brave song
Though they know the end is near.
The nights are getting colder
The days shorter though they still
Carry the heat of summer.
Every night for months now
I go to sleep by their pulsating song
That fills the air with sound.
Not beautiful yet comforting
In its strength and constancy.
As autumn progresses, a sadness
Can be felt and heard.
The cricket's song grows weaker,
Their numbers diminish.
The last night's song is the most beautiful
As if they know
Tonight we sing for all eternity.

* * *

Prairies and oceans,
What do they know
Of tumult and foreign shores?
Only the depths will hold
The secret of their crossing.

Do you know the secrets

Of the night and darkness?
All the hidden doings
Wrapped in velvet silence.
None dare speak of them.
Concealment perfectly rendered
Unto the Source of all things.

What is it to say
You will do what must be done?
Doing is always too late.
Being waits for your decision
To return to where you must be.
Any place less than that
Is deserted, empty, like ashes
After the fire has gone out.

The Silence can teach us much if we allow. Words can only go so far in their attempt to instruct and clarify. At the foundation of the world, of the mind, is a great Silence from which all sound arises. Sounds are effective in their attempt to communicate to the exact degree they contain the Silence which is intelligence. Intelligence is prior to words and concepts, being an attribute of Mind Itself. Thought is one of the actions of mind as is perception. Intelligence, if given the opportunity to function, orders and directs thought that it may be coherent and useful. The constant operation of thought, the continuous flow of thoughts, images, impulses and feelings, is simply the past appearing in the present as if it were now. The process of thought, in and of itself, is not of the present nor is it guided by intelligence. The chattering mind, as it is aptly named by some, lives by its own momentum and has its own rules that are not bound by logic and reason.

If one observes the mind carefully and consistently, it soon becomes apparent that the "you," whatever you take yourself to be, usually a person or thinking "entity," is not the source of this thought process nor do you have any control over its fundamental movement and its constant activity unless you attempt to direct the process, to join in for the purpose of focusing thought on a particular object or theme. If you have trained your mind to focus and reason, then you may be able to control the thought process for awhile to serve a purpose you have given it. As soon as you have accomplished your aim, however, and then turned your attention elsewhere, the chattering mind will regain its autonomy and once again will race ahead following its own dictates.

All of this can be quite easily and obviously observed by anyone willing to take the time and make the effort. There is nothing secret or mysterious about this activity which goes on all the time during your waking hours as even a modest attempt at self-awareness will confirm. If indeed the chattering mind operates beyond individual control or motivation, then clearly is your relationship to it very important as it can and does affect your life in major ways. The greatest mistake we can make is to believe what appears in our mind as "thinking" is true simply because we believe we are the source of these thoughts. Recently I came across a statement on a bumper sticker that expresses this idea very well: "Don't believe everything you think."

Human thinking is least effective as a response to life's problems when it is automatic, unreflective. If our thinking, be it individual or collective, arises from past habits and conditioning, if it contains unexamined biases or distortions, then is it very unlikely to be helpful in understanding issues or responding to the situations that confront us. The ability of mind to think about, to direct thought, to contemplate and consider, is an important part of our responses to the challenges of life. As such it is extremely important that our thinking response be as clear as possible of factors that cloud or distort our minds and thus reduce or obstruct our understanding. Making decisions that arise from incomplete or distorted understanding will be obviously limited at best and ineffective at worst.

What if the thinking "entity," call it what you will, were to become aware of the constant movement of thought flowing through the mind, yet were not absorbed in or identified with it? What if the individual, the "I," the self-awareness, recognized in a fundamental way that most thoughts don't really belong to him/her despite their apparently personal nature? This recognition, to whatever degree it develops, begins to free the self-awareness, the "I," from the chaos, distortions, and limitations of the autonomous thought process. Such a mind then has a chance to allow the real functioning of intelligence to arise in awareness and begin to direct and develop understanding that is based on Love and inclusion. Real understanding is only possible if the mind is in a state of peace and harmony. Fear, conflict and judgment make impossible the accurate perception and clear thinking that are needed to come to authentic understanding which alone can lead to appropriate and effective responses to life.

Since when does mind understand anything?
Can words wash away the pain
Of grief and sadness?
Do thoughts reveal to you
The truth of your own existence?
Symbols, sounds, internal and external
Poorly represent what exists beyond them.
They can be well used if
You understand their limits as
Pointers to what is beyond
The farthest reaches of mind.
Never more than this.

The Heart of all communicates
Directly to your heart.

No words, no feelings
Just communication of Being.
A Love that cannot be measured
A Light that never grows dim
Bliss without limits.
Heart is all, Love is all.
Communication whole and endless
Without beginning or end
Has always been.

Whatever happened to the art of thinking? Is thinking really allowed today? I am referring here to the act of thinking for yourself, of quietly examining something such as an idea or belief with an open mind, leaving bias and preconception behind as much as possible, and just letting the object of your contemplation reveal itself. There are limits to where thought can take you as it is always a secondhand, once removed function of mind. Always conceptual thinking, mentation, is removed from the object of its attention be that an event, an existence, an opinion, an idea etc., and thinking suffers from that distance be it a distance of kind or quality. Yet thinking is important and helpful if it is used rightly, and to use it rightly is to recognize its strengths and be aware of its weaknesses, i.e. its limitations.

The lack of awareness of the limitations of thinking is glaringly obvious in much of the intellectual discussion taking place nowadays in virtually all realms of human discourse. Thinking, intellectualizing, has been enthroned by many Western academics, intellectuals and self-appointed rationalists as the only means by which "truth" or "reality" can be ascertained or proven. This despite the fact that science does not rely on mere human thinking (though it is obviously a part of its methodology), but proves the truth of its hypotheses through observable experience, empirical evidence, and the use of mathematical tools. What is lost in the worship of the intellect is the wholeness of mind and its other capacities such as intuition, insight, and inspiration, to name a few, not to mention the least common of all things, common sense.

As mentioned elsewhere, intelligence itself is not a byproduct of thinking but stands prior to thought as it is a fundamental capacity of Mind and is not dependent on other attributes of mind for its existence. The use of the thought process can include intelligence, can be directed by it to some degree or not at all. Indeed, the degree to which intelligence is operating in the intellectual discourse of our time varies greatly and, in some cases, seems to be absent altogether. Mind as such, Mind in its Wholeness, is the home of intelligence, not the brain though intelligence can take up temporary residence there. In the Western approach to thinking, the use of concepts according to some of the rules of logic, concepts arranged in the form of a clever and consistent argument for or against something, is considered intelligence, i.e. using concepts and argument to prove or disprove, persuade or dissuade, is regarded as the expression of, the proof of intelligence. Thus is intelligence reduced to a certain clever use of verbal symbols; it is both linked to the use of words and proven by that use. Regarded as inseparable from either conceptual functioning or abstract reasoning (such as in mathematics, physics, and other sciences), intelligence appears to be a kind of secondary effect of consciousness, one that is linked to or identical with the activity of mind that we call thinking. Lost in this approach somehow is the relationship between intelligence and fact, between intelligence and the Wholeness of Life Itself.

Very clever arguments can be and are being made to justify and support the continuation of our economic system, for example, which is based on continuous and unending growth within a planetary system that has definite limits to growth. The earth is not infinitely capable of being the location of and source of raw materials and foodstuffs that support growth predicated on, to all intents and purposes, infinite increase. Very simple mathematical reasoning clearly shows the insanity of our economic expectations yet they are not seriously raised to question except by a very few who are not listened to. The great majority of educated people, experts, and economists support and benefit from our modern economy and will not look beyond it. Should this be considered intelligence? Is it intelligent to add more fuel to the fire and increase the speed at which the Titanic is approaching the iceberg? Is it intelligence to focus so much time and energy on rearranging the deck chairs when you should be running for the lifeboats?

Surely intelligence should have some relationship to the actual facts of life, those rather inconvenient circumstances that surround us. To paraphrase Mark Twain: there is something that trumps logic and clever arguments, and that is fact. You cannot argue with a fact, you cannot argue with the law of gravity. It is what it is and will have its effect whether we admit it or not. Facts stand by themselves; they do not enter into the realm of argument for or against. They are not affected by it. The relationship of argument to fact is only in the interpretation of it. Here is where many erroneous arguments began.

Interpretation of anything starts with the value system of the interpreter. Ideas of good and bad, gain and loss, not to mention ingrained biases that are a part of our belief system: all these color and direct the interpretation of a fact. Coherent response to a fact begins with the admission of its existence. Then follows the projection of interpretation, which hopefully leads to understanding and right response if a response is needed.

How can anything be understood
If the instrument by which
It is measured is cloudy, defective?
The one instrument always at your disposal
The mind, your very own mind.

All understanding comes through mind,
Is determined by the action of mind.
Mind does many things – observe,
Project, think, deduct, reason
Analyze, synthesize, summarize, conclude.
All may be used to help understanding
If used rightly.

Mind is the tool when used well
Can solve all problems capable of solution
And make right decisions
For those that are not.
The usefulness of mind depends on
The understanding of it.
A tool to be useful must be
Correctly applied and good will result.
Misapplied it will lead you astray.
Its power can be used
To help or hinder.

The purpose of mind most fundamentally is to be aware, to be conscious. All other actions and functions of mind arise in the basic awareness and take place within it. Awareness can be said to be the context, the background, in which, against which, the content of mind – thoughts, feelings, perceptions, impulses, desires, images etc. – appear and fulfill their function. All these are secondary attributes of mind because they do not exist outside of awareness while awareness itself is present with or without content. This is perhaps not so apparent to the everyday, constantly chattering mind that never seems to be devoid of content, but can be experienced in meditative states of consciousness which are attainable by anyone who is willing to quiet and train the mind sufficiently. As the great majority of people especially in our busy, restless, modern society do not experience the quiet mind in which simple awareness is not obscured by constant mental activity, this most basic condition and quality of mind goes unnoticed. Consequently life itself, understanding, and decision making are dominated by the more or less unrestrained, continuous thought process and the conditioning influence of upbringing, social environment, and education that drive it.

What do you really know?
Do you know what you think you know?
How do you know what you know?
Do not mistake belief for knowledge,
To believe is not to know.
Belief is opinion based on desire.
We believe what we want to believe,
This is never in question.
Do you want to believe
What is true?
Then you must go beyond
Desire, bias, opinion, comfort,
Learn to inquire and observe.
Above all, learn to observe
Your own mind in action.
Watch its movements, feel what lies
Behind them, what moves thought.

Motivation is often not understood
Yet always it drives our minds
And colors our thinking.
Clever arguments, logic, reason
Often have a starting point unexamined.
A line of thought is as sound as
The assumptions on which it rests.
When these assumptions are unconscious,

Unexamined, then thinking rests upon
Instability, shifting sands, nothingness.
Nothing of value can be built
Without a firm foundation.
All true understanding arises from
A clear and empty awareness,
A Wholeness that does not exclude
The reality of experience.

Thinking has its place but
Without a grounding in its source,
Without an origin in clarity and silence,
Thinking is like a kite blown about
By the winds of emotion
Without a tail, untethered to
The ground of experience.
Amusing it may be, entertaining maybe,
Stimulating for those with time to waste,
No more than that.

The heart is where it all begins and where it ends. The origin of all is Love, the Heart of Love. Without Love there is no true beginning, just the continuation of meaninglessness. All activity, be it thought, feeling, speech or behavior, that is not rooted in Love, is devoid of true meaning. The endless busyness of mind and body arise from the opposition to Love's Presence. Fear rides the rails of much of human endeavor. It drives development and change, permeates the movement of "progress" and human society in general, and is carrying us on to an unknown future. The positive elements of our civilization are theoretically aiming to build a better and better society; motivated by a kind of utopian ideal, they are attempting to engineer and direct change which they hope will create a good life for all, a life in which poverty, uncertainty and violence will be eliminated.

Yet the question remains: Is it possible to do away with uncertainty in human life? Is it possible or even desirable to attempt to develop complete control over our physical circumstances? Yes it is good to make life comfortable to a great degree as is the case for many in the developed world; it is good to eliminate human suffering of all kinds to the degree that can be accomplished. Unfortunately, the means by which we accomplish this may also bring their own set of problems. Our way of food production, for example, has given the human race the capability to banish starvation, malnutrition, and famine from human experience. Yet these problems persist, even in the rich countries to some degree, and in the developing world they are endemic. Human and economic factors prevent food from reaching all and population growth further complicates the problem. Even if these factors could be corrected and sufficient food made available to all, significant problems would remain. Soil loss and erosion due to intensive farming practices make current production unsustainable in the long run. The chemicals that are used in modern agriculture have polluted the water supply in many areas and this will only get worse. These chemicals also poison our bodies and can cause cancer and other possible life-threatening conditions. The uncertainty of the food supply is being controlled using means that increase the uncertainty of human health.

A careful consideration of many of the factors of modern life that have improved the conditions in which we live reveals a startling fact. Many modern discoveries are like the proverbial double-edged sword that cuts both ways. On the one hand, they may solve a problem or bring some kind of improvement to the human condition. On the other hand, they may create another problem or contribute to already existing ones. We are increasingly finding ourselves in a situation of can't live without them and can't live with them, damned if we do and damned if we don't. I'm not going to go into details here. I leave that to the reader who is willing to look around at life and think about these things.

Autumn has come to the desert, bringing with it all the changes reflected in nature. The blue of the sky is softer, gentler. As the sun sinks lower towards the south, its light is not so harsh, its rays not so warming. The wind is cooler, bringing a hint of the cold weather to come. The crickets' song still fills the night but it is muted, softer than during the summer. Along the river, the cattails are fully ready to abandon their tiny seeds with their down-like parachutes to the mercy of the winds. The river is very relaxed, with a sleepy, slow-moving current carrying the light green water onward to its rendezvous with the Great Colorado. The bright yellow of the leaves on the cottonwoods, the sleepy green water, the straw-colored tall grass, the soft blue sky and the gentle late afternoon sunlight, each complete in itself, somehow blend together, a delicate, spontaneous beauty that is more than the sum of its parts. The Wholeness of Life is there, its fragility and the constant flow of change, birth, growth, and death. Yet in that is death only a part of it all, not an ending. Death is just one part of the constant transformation of form, color, and creation. Death leads to life again, and life changes form in death only to reappear again and again to continue the dance that never ends.

Whenever you feel lost, alone
Remember there is a Friend,
One who walks with you
Who will never forsake you.
The footsteps you hear may be your own
Yet surrounded by love you need not fear.
Sustained and protected, you journey on,
The ground beneath your feet blessed
By the Holy Ones who have gone before.
Some day you will look in the mirror

And see the Holiness that is you.
Until that day keep pretending,
Do not recognize your Self.
Remain a weary figure
Trudging along earth's dusty roads.
Follow your shadow till you tire
Of ignorance and self-deception.
Ask for help and look within.
Let the Light in the heart
Speak through its shining.
The mind must be taught
How to see and recognize
What cannot be seen, only known.
Knowing will release the power
Within and the power of Love
Will take you home.

Whenever you ask for help, it is given you. To receive it, you must accept it to know it is there. The help from on high may come in many ways: from without or within, through your surroundings or directly into your mind. In order to accept anything you must know it is there; it must be recognized. The mind absorbed in the constant chatter of thought is not available to the present. Only in the present can authentic guidance and help be recognized and received.

Willingness is required to accomplish anything, and also focused intent. The mind is quite capable of learning if you direct it appropriately; and repetition is a fundamental learning principle. Again and again must the mind be turned towards the goal. The unruly mind will resist the attempts to bring it to a state of quiet as anyone who has ever attempted meditation has discovered. Only when the mind is calm and quiet can you discover what waits for the mind and heart to open that the gifts of Spirit may be given you.

How long have you walked
Many paths that lead nowhere
But to your death?
You have breathed the choking dust
As the winds of chaos swirl all around you,
Longing for the pure air
Of the heights of Spirit.
Looking upwards towards the mountains high
Clothed in purest light,
Your heart reaches out
But cannot touch that stillness.
The valley's clamor, busy figures
Racing about, going nowhere fast
Seem to sweep you along,
To surround you with their busyness.

Heedless of the beauty that calls
To them from above,
They will not raise their gaze
Which remains fixed on the next step
Before them and the next and the next.
In like manner, they continue
Unwilling to see the present
That waits for them to notice.

The future you seek never comes.
It is a phantom, a mirage
Beckoning to you from beyond
The horizon of everyday life.
Chasing shadows will never satisfy
Your need for the Real.
Neither future nor past can contain
The Reality that moves the present
And contains all that is

Or was or ever will be.

It seems to me the last thing the human mind wants to hear is a simple, direct statement of truth that cuts through the complexity of human thinking, a complexity that is all too often meaningless and unnecessary. In our era, many of us "educated" ones seem to prefer to assume a basic position of doubt that looks upon life from a perspective unwilling to know or determine what is true or real in the most basic sense, and prefers endless arguments and speculation instead. This attitude is both self-perpetuating and self-defeating. It's a mystery to me why so many otherwise intelligent people limit the use of their mind to such useless conceptualizing.

Life itself is not conceptual; it is not all the words we use to describe or analyze or react to it. The fact of our existence and our fundamental awareness that we exist is prior to thought and independent of it. With that fact in mind, it is possible to place the thinking process in a better perspective, i.e. not to assign to it the exclusive role of determining truth or untruth but rather recognize thinking as one of several functions of mind that can be useful in that regard. In the Eastern spiritual traditions it is said that the intellect is a good servant but a bad master. Here in the West, however, there is a tendency to worship, to idolize intellectualizing, conceptualizing, and overestimate its usefulness and applicability. Better a balanced use of every tool in the mental toolbox than an unbalanced and exaggerated use of one to the exclusion or detriment of all others.

The questions of life most in need of meaningful answers cannot be reduced to mere mental projections derived from what one wants to believe. There is a Reality to Which we all belong and in Which we live and have our being. The fundamental task of life is not to make up our own answers and then spend our time trying to convince ourselves and others that these answers are true. Our fundamental responsibility is to discover the answers that await our recognition because they are true and universal. The Truth is the Truth because it's true and nothing else is true. This has always been the case and always will be. The conceptual mind is the realm of conflict, contradiction, and change. In Truth, there is no conflict, contradiction, or change. The transient, relative sphere of existence is where we struggle with the problem of opposites. Time and space are predicated upon separation and change, conflict and difference. These are unavoidable aspects of the time/space continuum and the defense of individual identity.

There is a way to step beyond the limitations of conceptual thought and reach a state of certainty even though all about you may be lost in confusion and uncertainty. Paradoxically, you must begin by accepting the fact that you know nothing. All you think you have learned in the past must be put aside that the mind may become empty, open, and surrendered. The state of uncertainty that characterizes the mind of ignorance arises from its attempt to find certainty where it cannot be found. The world around us in which we live does not include the possibility of certainty. All things here are temporary, passing phenomena. Everything is in a state of constant change, constant flux. Human life is marked by frequent change which has reached a fever pitch in the current era due to the ever-increasing rate of change in our technological development and the widespread economic and political instability around the globe. Certainty cannot be obtained while you are standing on quicksand.

Reliance on what is seen
On what is perceived as if
This could be depended upon
Will leave you stranded
On a foreign shore. The waves
Of change will batter
The walls of every house

You construct.

Water, wind, and fire,
Impersonal forces of nature
Are no respecters of persons
Or property. No one knows
When change will come or where.
The body itself, constantly changing
With the passing of time,
Growing, gaining, losing, aging
Eventually crumbling into dust
Or consigned to the flames.
Is anything less reliable than this?

This masquerade of emptiness,
Costumed images that come and go
Appearing in the mirror of awareness
Cannot affect the one who witnesses.
Identification with the temporary,
With the parade of passing events
Imprisons you in a cage
Of your own making.
Reject the role of jailor
You have assigned yourself.
Your last act will be
To open the cage door
And watch the return of freedom.

Freedom cannot be yours
While you relish imprisonment.
Conditions may be quite comfortable
And amusing here in central jail.
The windows are gaily painted
To hide the iron bars.

Though they are only in the mind
They appear all around you.
No matter where you go
The road before you is blocked.
All roads on earth lead nowhere.
Realize that and the way
Will open before you and you will
Know and find your way home.

If you are willing to leave behind all you think you know, then is the mind ready and willing to learn what must be done. It is impossible to learn when the mind is filled with the self-importance of belief. Belief in and of itself is neither good nor bad. What matters is the relationship of a belief system to Truth. What supports and points to Truth is helpful. What reinforces and multiplies illusion is not. There is a very human tendency to defend one's beliefs often at the expense of truth. The mind believes in what it has made and identifies with it. Thus to have one's belief system questioned is often interpreted as an attack, and attack is always met with defense and often counterattack. The conflict that arises between differing belief systems is extremely difficult to resolve because of the investment of personal identity in what we believe to be true whether the belief is of a political nature, social nature, or be it about the nature of reality and the meaning of life. The deep emotional attachment to our beliefs in general and some of them in particular, such as beliefs around politics or religion, make reasonable dialogue and discussion very difficult, hence the increasing polarity of our society in very fundamental ways. A spirit of good will, tolerance, and fairness, combined with a touch of humility and the recognition of the limits of our individual knowledge, would be very helpful at this time in both public and private discourse.

To think you know everything

Is to know nothing.
Ignorance is seldom silent
Quick to flaunt its opinions.
Truth is buried under a barrage
Of useless verbiage.
Silent awareness is the home
Of those who know peace.
Agitation of mind obscures
Clear thinking like gray clouds
Hide the sky above.
The task of those who would
Know themselves is to clear
The mind of all that is
Useless, obscure, and unnecessary.

The constant inner noise of
The wandering mind drowns out
The still, small voice of Truth.
Truth does not oppose or
Fight to be heard.
It merely waits until you
Are ready to listen.
Speaking simply, directly, to those
Who would hear and understand,
Everything is revealed, is given
At its appointed time
To the mind ready to receive
And use what is given.

* * *

Whither goest thou?
A question not easily answered.
"I'm going to the store."

Is it that simple?
Toys, shiny baubles, so many
Exciting items to buy and
Carry home and revel in their
Possession. What profiteth it you
To gain the whole world if by
So doing you lose communication
With your own Soul, the Essence
From which, by which, you live?
Does your journey of life
Lead down many shopping aisles
Through the emporiums of pleasure
The rows of fine houses and big yards,
Past the numerous places of distraction
And entertainment? Do you seek pleasure
And escape in the many substances available
For that purpose? A life devoted
To comfort and stimulation, pleasures
Of all sorts, and the acquisition
Of possessions, amassing material wealth
Or the exercise of ambition, goals
Pursued, honors received, fame
And adulation; is this your choice?
All men and women are
Created equal but all lives are
Not created equal. Each of us
Creates our life based on what we
Do and don't do, what we value,
What we include and exclude.
Where we put our energy and
Effort, there our heart is also.
The factors of time:
Money, wealth and possessions.
The attainments of time: honors,

Achievements, fame, knowledge
And skill, all will pass away,
Vanish down the dusty corridors
Of time leaving nothing
But the present, ever new
Reborn each moment, calling
You to live here, to live now
Rather than dream your life
Away chasing glittering phantoms
That are without value or substance.
Life itself will not be televised.
Eventually all the long running programs
That make up your life,
Will be cancelled, the digital fog
Will lift, and on a brand new day
You will realize that you
Can see forever.

Man is the meeting point of various stages of Reality.
Rudolph Eucken

Chapter 7

Mind and the Dream

What price are you willing to pay to ransom life from the limitations you have imposed on it? The security blanket of the past, its habits and memories, grows thinner with every passing year. A time will come when the choice will present itself, to wrap the tattered past ever more tightly about your mind, or to throw it off, leave it lying in the road behind you and walk on fearlessly into the light of a new day. This choice may be postponed for years, centuries, eons, but it will not go away. It walks with you patiently waiting, waiting till you are ready.

Is not the everyday life you experience like a dream? Things happen "accidentally" for no rhyme or reason. Events occur seemingly randomly and affect few or many. Though everyday life is more ordered, predictable, and consistent than our nightly dreams, there is nonetheless always the element of the random, the beyond our controlness, that is present in life on all levels from the individual to the collective. Despite the best efforts of modern civilization to impose control over all the factors of existence, we are still falling well short of our goal. In actuality, many of the control mechanisms based on technology bring with them unforeseen consequences that are themselves difficult or impossible to control; consequences that increase the range of random and unforeseen events and the uncertainty of physical life.

The deepest discoveries of science, of physics, have revealed a world that is, in very basic ways, not at all what we perceive and experience as the world of everyday life. What could be more dreamlike and surreal than to see things as they are not and experience a stability and repetitiveness that is not there? The place where we live, the environment that surrounds us seems to be firm, stable, unmoving. It is we who move around upon it and through it. In truth, the entire earth is moving at a speed of many thousands of miles an hour through space as it follows its predetermined course around our sun. The earth is also moving in a circular motion around its central axis, a distance of about twenty-five thousand miles every twenty-four hours, a little more than a thousand miles an hour. From your local frame of reference, you may wake up in the same bed, the same house and the same neighborhood, city or town, state, country, and continent every morning, but your entire location, carrying you with it, is in a different "cosmic" neighborhood than yesterday morning, a different region of space, more than a million miles removed from yesterday.

Time is an illusion, vast and mysterious, a sleight of hand. No one can say just what it is. Perhaps it can be described as the backdrop of change, that which allows change to happen. Change is measured by the difference observed in a quantity or quality (i.e. amount, electromagnetic charge, position relative to a starting point, color, size etc.) over time. Without time there is no change and without change there is no time. They appear inseparable, certainly in the practical sense. Time is not uniform nor is it unaffected by circumstances as Einstein proved with his Special Theory of Relativity. The faster you travel through space, the slower the passage of time for you. If it were possible to move at the speed of light, as you reach the speed of light, time for you would stop.

Remember last night out among
The stars that glittered overhead
As you lay on the sacred earth
Wrapped in a warm blanket?
Hungry and thirsty, you could not
Sleep. Around you was the
Sound of chanting, deep voices

That seemed close yet far away.
And you understood those voices
Calling you from the ancient
Depths of time, reminding you
Of what you once were and would be again.

Your answer does not matter.
To say no is to postpone
In time what will happen
Anyway. The ancient ones
Cannot be refused. They wait.
Civilizations come and go.
Empires rise, flourish, then fall.
All things return to dust
Then rise to live again.
When you tire of this
Parade of changing forms
And fortunes, you will become
Part of this chanting.

Do you know who you are? Not the you with a name, photo ID, with a past and a projected future, a vacation, a car, a home of some kind, a bank account, and a mind full of ideas and beliefs, likes and dislikes, desires and aversions; that is not what I am referring to. I am referring to the sense of self-awareness, of being, the fundamental I am, I exist, I am aware and I am aware that I am aware. Who is the fundamental you that is almost buried beneath the details of your life, the activities and busyness, the chattering mind that never stops?

Socrates, the ancient Greek philosopher, teacher of Plato, said long ago, "The unexamined life is not worth living." Contrast that with the modern slogan, "The unexamined life is the only life worth living." If you were living a life which included a very fundamental soul-searching type examination of your own mind, your thinking, motives and values, if you looked deeply into what you believe, what you think you know, how you reach your conclusions that lead to belief and presumed knowledge: would you be living the same life as your present existence?

Most of us are living in a way that has been handed down to us by the past. Our parents, educational institutions, social pressure, the media and the advertising to which we have been exposed, have taught us the pattern of life we follow. Despite all the hoopla of a "free society" and the ideal of self-expression, doing it "my way" etc., life for many, even most, is derivative, shaped by all the influences that surround us and very predictable. So-called free expression is limited mostly to how you choose to get intoxicated via various substances and who you have sex with. Even here the grooves in which most of us are moving have been laid down for us by the past. What is most lacking in so many lives is a sense of authenticity. Life is more and more like a mediocre reality show, a long-running repeat of the basic human themes of work, play, love, hate, stimulation and sex, intoxication, vacations and shopping. Children are born and introduced to the same quality of existence as their parents, and the entire movement of life is overlaid by the digital fog which consumes the attention of so many as they focus on the little screen in their hands and the act of communicating the banal details of everyday life to whoever will listen. The consumer culture is brilliantly designed to cater to our weaknesses and habitual tendencies; brain-numbing advertising continually comes at us through every possible medium. The soundtrack of modern life is a constant blare of commercials encouraging us to buy, buy, buy.

Can authenticity be found among all the temptations that surround us? When all you know is what is presented to you to buy, when entertainment is continually dangled before your eyes, and comfort, ease, and affluence have become the central purpose of your life: is it possible to find authentic meaning? A mind blinded by desire and ambition, obsessed with pleasure and comfort, living only on the surface of things, simply responding to what is put in front of it, living reactively rather than creatively: can such a mind discover the deeper dimensions of life where real meaning waits? We give our life the meaning it has for us. We invest our goals and conditions with value, a value we choose according to our biases and tendencies.

Yet life is given us, we are a part of it. We have not created ourselves or the life that is all around us. Meaning is inherent in life itself; it need not be invented and superimposed based on our shifting states, experiences, and desires. The meaning of life does not change over time; like its Source, true meaning is rooted in the eternal and is reflected in time, giving our lives their purpose and value. Yes, we can assign our own purpose, determine our own value for what we want to do, but unless they are in accordance with universal meaning, they are not helpful and may even have a negative effect on our lives. An invented meaning, a self-determined purpose; these will never take the place of what is universal and true. There are no substitutes for Truth. One of our tasks in life is to discover, to realize the inherent meaning, the purpose of life, that waits for our recognition and acceptance. We are not expected to invent or make up a meaningful purpose. Indeed, to do so is to obscure that which is waiting for us to discover.

The eagle does not struggle
To reach the sky.
Its flight is a gift
Carried within, waiting for
The time of readiness.
When the moment comes,
It spreads its wings and
Leaps into the abyss.
The only thing required

Is the courage to leap.
The strength of its wings,
The wind that carries it,
All is given already.
Do not cling to the nest
When the time to fly has come.

I was sitting on the front porch of my home, enjoying the early morning, when a blackbird suddenly flew over to me, hovered about six feet above my head making a harsh squawking sound for several seconds, then flew across the road and hovered above a spot about fifty feet away in the empty field beside the road. After a few seconds, the bird came back, repeated its behavior, then returned to hover above the same spot in the empty field as before. When it repeated this action for a third time, I realized it was telling me something; it was trying to draw my attention to the empty field across the road for some reason.

So I stood up and walked over to where the blackbird was still hovering about twelve feet above the ground. The field was covered by a large fishing net composed of many fine strands of some kind of plastic or nylon. The net was often spread out there to dry by the man and wife who lived beside the road on the other side in an old house whose walls and fences were randomly decorated with shells, driftwood, and occasional pieces of fishing equipment. They were professional fishermen, and used the large net among other things to make their living. As I came close to the spot above which the blackbird was hovering, I saw a second blackbird, a female, on the ground. Clearly she was his mate and her feet had become tangled in the strands of the net, leaving her trapped on the ground unable to fly. As I knelt beside her, she tried repeatedly to leap into the air and fly away. Concerned that she might break a leg or otherwise injure herself in her desperation to escape, I took her gently into my hand and held her fast. She stopped her struggles and became motionless.

Reaching down I gently unwound the strands that clung to her feet until they suddenly fell off leaving her feet free. I opened my hand and she leaped into the air, and with a final squawk from her mate who had arranged the rescue, they quickly flew off.

This is an amazing example of one of the wild creatures who share our life on this earth asking for help with a situation that was a matter of life and death for his mate. The blackbird had recognized a problem that he could not solve, and he understood that a human creature could help. All he needed to do was get my attention and point out the exact spot where his mate was trapped. To this day I still remember his concern, his ability to communicate to me the dire situation, and the intelligence behind his actions.

All living creatures are part of the Great Intelligence that permeates the universe. Intelligence takes different forms according to the physical structure of the individual organism. It may be a very simple intelligence or very complex and developed such as with human beings. What is regarded as intelligence is a faculty or aspect of Consciousness Itself. As all life has consciousness, all life also has intelligence. In human society, intelligence is defined and measured by mental functions such as verbal ability, abstract reasoning, comprehension of verbal instructions etc.; intelligence is much more than that. It cannot be reduced to mental activity no matter how clever or complex. The true range of intelligence cannot be measured by our tests or limited by our beliefs and imagination. Intelligence is much more than the mental exercise of verbal or abstract thinking.

The sun has set
And the land grows dark.
A chill in the air
Warns us winter is coming.
The grass is dry, brittle, like straw.

Time for those who must
Sleep the winter through
To find their refuge, their bed.
The snow will come later.
For now, falling leaves and
The death of flowers
Tell us to be ready,
To prepare for the harsh times
That are coming.

The sun sets on the rich
And the poor, the governed
And those who govern.
It looks upon empires
And the ruins of empires.
Everything arises, grows
Has its day in the sun.
All things pass away
When their time is over.
That is the way of the world.
No use to mourn what has gone,
Open to the new day that is coming.

If there is no way to be what you are, you will be something
else. Not because you would rather be other than what you are,
but because you must be something, must have an identity. The
mind is afraid of being nothing; it must be something, and if true
identity has been lost, it will invent an image and invest it with
belief. Thus does a personal identity arise which believes itself
to be a body, an image, and this identification with a projected
image makes it impossible for the memory of true existence, so
long forgotten, to return.

What sets one thing off from another is the apparent
differences that mark each. Differences are always of quantity

and/or quality. They are differences of form, of perception, and as such are characteristics of form and function, what we can call the outer. Always it is the outer, physically perceivable aspects of things that we observe, relate to and measure. The outer, the obvious, the surface of things, is thought to be by many the reality, the "truth" of their existence.

Overlooked in this estimation and relationship with what appears around us is the inwardness, the inner dimension of life. I am not referring here to a spatial quality such as the inner space of the human body, i.e. the abdominal cavity, the chest cavity etc. There is a more basic aspect to the inner, one that has to do with Being Itself, with Consciousness Itself, not with its content – dualistic perception, thoughts, feelings, impulses, images etc. This inner Beingness is not an individualized quality or characteristic as is the case with the outer world of form and perception. Being is universal and is One. It includes all apparent individuality within it as Essence. The Essence of all energy and force is Light; the Essence of all mind is pure Consciousness Itself, and the Essence of all apparent existence in form is Beingness.

Is it difficult to realize
Life's vastness does not depend
On time or space or measurement?
Close your eyes. Where is
The universe now? Where did it go?
You hold it in memory, nowhere else.
So vast your mind, it can hold
What cannot be seen or measured effortlessly.

Mind is all there is. Everything around you is mind or its content. The power of Mind to create is absolute. No other power exists but Mind. Mind is the agent, the functional power of Spirit, supplying Its creative energy, Light, Which is the ultimate Source of all the forms of energy we experience in the physical world.

Individual mind shines by means of a reflected light that is not its own though it seems to be. The One Universal Mind is aware through each and every seeming fragment of Itself that appears as separate form. Life as a separate entity, seemingly capable of making its own choices and acting independently of the world that surrounds it, seems very convincingly real, does it not? Consequently, the reality of what we seem to be and experience is never brought into question. Experience brings conviction, and repeated and consistent experience solidifies that conviction.

It can be argued that all experience will be limited and partial. As there is a huge range of possible experience available at any time in this state of conscious life, and at any one moment no individual experiences more than a tiny part of it, clearly then is individual experience of life partial and limited. Even if you were to add up all the moments of experience in any one lifetime, the sum total would still be a very, very, almost immeasurably small part of the total movement of life around us, in us, and through us. Thus it can be said that our conviction of the reality of our experience as seemingly separate and independent form is based on a very small slice of the total possible experience of life. Despite that, however, there is a tendency of mind to generalize from its limited taste of existence and impose that generalization not just on all of life around it, but also include in its imposition all the possibilities, the potentials of experience. By so doing, however, we are passing judgment on the nature of Reality Itself, be that judgment conscious or unconscious, and are imposing limits on the possibilities of experience itself, limits that keep our mind within the narrow containment of past experience.

The continuum of consciousness is virtually unlimited in its scope and intelligence. It cannot be captured within the narrow boundaries of human belief systems. Consciousness is that within which human belief systems are formulated through the action of thought, the conditioning influences that act upon thought, and the emotions that drive the direction of thought. All too often human belief is simply a justification of prevalent biases regardless of what is true or false. So long as the human mind continues to be unaware of its own dynamics, of how it works, and unaware of its deep content, or, to be a little more accurate, in denial of what has been called its shadow side, so long will conflict dominate human relations at all levels, and the inevitable result of conflict, violence and injustice will continue to cast their dark shadow across human life. The dark side of the personality, as it has been called, contains the repressed, the unacknowledged, the forgotten trauma, pain, fear, rage, and hatred. These powerful emotions, these memories and their energetic charge do not go away because we are no longer aware of them. They remain in the mind below the threshold of conscious awareness, influencing and distorting our conscious thinking, feeling, and the thought processes in general.

A shepherd walks down a dusty road
Leading his sheep to pasture.
They know not where they go
Yet trust the one who leads.
Are we not like that?
Who knows where they go
What will happen tomorrow?
Does that prevent you today
From fulfilling your duty?
Loving, giving, working, and doing
What must be done?
Tomorrow is unknown and
The day after even more so.
Next week is shrouded in mystery
Next year like a strange country.

The future ever evades expectation,
Waiting for us to arrive
Surprising us with its gifts
Or taking away what we have.
Here one day, gone the next,
Even your body may not
Be here tomorrow.

There is no substitute for God as our Creator. Many, many ideas are there about what God is or what God wants; many images of God have been constructed, defended, and elaborated on. No image constructed by the human mind captures the Truth of what God is. God is Love, God is the Source of all, are helpful ideas that point to the Reality that is the Creator. Yet it must be admitted that God cannot be grasped by human thought or reasoning; the Creator cannot be reduced to human mentation or emotion or belief. Thus is the conflict between religions, sects, and belief systems over the nature of God, what God wants of us, who has access to God etc., a kind of absurdity, an absurdity that has its origin in human mental processes and the emotional attachment to belief systems. Since the beliefs regarding God also include beliefs about the nature and purpose of the individual, of human life, and the meaning of life, all very deep core beliefs, the religious thought system is heavily defended. For most, the beliefs they hold about the nature of reality, i.e. religion among other things, are heavily invested in emotionally and thus are fertile ground for anger, conflict, and disagreement.

The need to argue and fight about anything including religion or the lack of it is grounded in the uncertainty that underlies belief systems. What we believe, organized into a configuration of sorts, is the mind's attempt to find stability and control in a world that appears to be outside us and beyond our control, even threatening at times. The mind believes in what it has made and identifies it as part of itself. A disagreement that contradicts, that seems to invalidate what the mind has invented and identified with, is perceived as an attack on itself. Attack will inevitably elicit fear, anger, defense, and counterattack from the one who feels attacked. Once this dynamic begins, real discourse becomes impossible.

All the discord between members of different religions has nothing to do with God, who has been widely and wisely perceived as beyond the human arena of hatred and violence, at least in recent years, by those not consumed by the flames of hatred. And let us not forget, the same dynamic of conflict and possible violence plays out among those who follow different political systems, among nations, among different tribal and ethnic groups, and at times between those of different socioeconomic classes. The source of these conflicts is the same regardless of the form of disagreement that precipitates the conflict.

The human mind carries deep within it the seeds of discord and hatred. What has been called the ego, the separate and separative sense of identity, of being a body, a separate and independent entity, existing in a context of many and varied separate entities and objects, and concerned mainly with its own safety and self-fulfillment, even, if necessary, at the expense of others: this is the fertile ground from which conflict arises. Many different avenues can channel or direct the sense of selfishness and separation from others, as well as the vague sense of threat also inherent in the ego mind, towards conflict with those who share life with us yet believe differently.

If you observe the human mind, yours and the minds around you over time, you will notice there is a need to judge others in most of us, even to the point of needing scapegoats on which to project blame and anger. The anger many people feel towards politicians, especially the President, is a good example. Our belief in the sins of others is a very obvious aspect of human thinking; very few of us apply the same rigorous standards by

which we judge and condemn others to ourselves. We often
condemn others for what we would overlook or justify in our
own case.

The pursuit of power over others
No matter the form or circumstance
Corrupts and defiles the mind
And heart. Love seeks not
To control or take away,
Love only gives and is helpful.
To give and receive are
Unavoidably linked. If you
Would not give, if you
Would only take, you are
Out of balance with the law
That governs life. All action
Has consequences good or bad.
Everything we do sets the law
In motion. Results are often
Not immediate but they will come.
Balance, sharing, giving, support life
Taking, controlling, suppressing, are anti-life
What opposes life leads to death.

* * *

The dance of existence
The unceasing ebb and flow
Over time, in space, fluctuates
Through the seasons, across eons.
Birth, life, and death alternate unceasingly
Change is constant, consistency
In change the pattern that determines
Life's expression. Again and again

It repeats, always the same
Yet always different. The river
Continues to flow, the water that
Flows is always new
Never yesterday, always now.
Be the one who dances
With life, through life, as life.
See yourself as you are
Not as you think or imagine
Yourself to be. The image, the person
Is a fiction superimposed on the river
Like a pattern drawn on flowing water.
It will not last. Death destroys
All superficial patterns. It cannot touch
The flowing waters of life that carry
All patterns for a little while.
Patterns come and go but
The waters of life flow forever.

What is meant by the word, the concept, practical? You may have often received in your life the advice to be practical. Just what does that mean? Obviously, like most concepts it can mean different things to different people and can vary depending on circumstances. Yet there is a kind of basic meaning or context in which the term "practical" is often used. Most often the concept is used in the context of material considerations: the physical conditions of life, economic security etc. If the concept of what is practical is applied to the economic sphere in general, our economy as a whole, then what is practical is generally understood and accepted as being what supports the continuous economic growth that is necessary to provide the means of material well-being for the greatest number of people. Underlying this assumption of course is the belief that a certain level of material well-being is necessary for people to be happy and be good citizens, not to mention the belief that material well-being must be accomplished through consumerism – the continuous consumption of goods and services without ceasing.

These assumptions, these beliefs, are accepted without question and heavily defended by just about everyone including the "experts" whose opinions are so heavily relied upon in the decision making and functioning of our civilization. Yet, as has been repeatedly stated in these pages, is an idea, a belief, practical or reasonable if it ignores some of the actual consequences that arise from its application; consequences that have a major impact on human life? The steadily and inexorably increasing degradation and pollution of the earth and the destruction of her natural systems is the immediate consequence of an economic system whose appetite for raw materials is voracious and unceasing, and whose byproducts from the invention of new technologies and the manufacturing of countless toys, gadgets, and widgets as well as the items considered indispensable to modern life are, in many cases, highly toxic to all life including humans.

Is it practical to poison yourself and destroy the basis on which your life and the economy depend, i.e. the natural world? Is mass suicide a practical response? Is it practical to employ large numbers of people to build a massive gallows and then hang everybody on it? Without a planet whose air is breathable and water drinkable, whose living systems support life, is there any such thing as an economy? The modern mind has removed itself so far from nature, lives in such an artificial environment, that it confuses virtual reality with the reality upon which it depends for its very existence. For many, nature is that quaint place they visit on weekends or during their vacation, a sort of unofficial theme park.

When birds no longer sing
And fish forget to swim,

The waters flow brown and polluted
And every morning you awake to silence,
What will you do then?
When the hills are bare of trees
And the forests are dying,
When the streams all dry up
And the refuse spills across the countryside,
What will you do then?
When those that came before you
Return to walk the barren earth
Their footsteps echoing like memories
Along the dusty, empty streets
When they gather silently about you
And look sadly into your eyes
What will you do then?

When the great forests are gone
And all the rivers are dammed,
The water beneath the earth
Drained by the great wells,
When the topsoil has all dried up
And blown away,
What will you do then?

When the great cities grow silent
Their busy throngs vanished into the past,
The blinking neon lights cease
Their messages of buy and sell,
The neighborhoods dark and deserted
And the few hide in the shadows
Or scurry across the rubble,
When being human no longer
Has meaning or purpose,
What will we do then?

The spirits of the vanished ones
Still linger in the wild places
Watching over the ruins
Their people had built
And inhabited so long ago.
The ceremonies continue though
We cannot see them or hear
The steady drumbeats and the chanting
That is all around us.
The medicine power waits,
Waits for those who are worthy
Who understand the old ways
Of Love for the Earth Mother
Respect for all life and
Respect for all our relations.

The plants and animals
Give their life that we may live.
Without gratitude there is
No respect. Without respect
There is no balance.
When we lay waste to the earth,
Refusing to acknowledge the debt
We owe to She who sustains
And nurtures all life including our own,
We cease to respect ourselves.

If the rhythm of life gets too far out of balance, the natural processes that are a part of that rhythm are also affected. All living things have a rhythm, a pattern of functioning that includes the pace of activity both internal and external, and an ebb and flow of the activities that characterize individual existence. This is also true for human life whether taking place in a simple agrarian setting or unfolding within a crowded and frantic city environment that includes a large population densely packed together.

What is beauty? Is it symmetry, proportion, shape, color, or curvature? What makes some things beautiful? Is it rightness, wholeness, emotion? It has been said that beauty is in the eye of the beholder. If that were true then there is no one standard by which beauty can be measured. What one culture finds beautiful is not so perceived by another culture. Music, for example, varies greatly from one culture to another, and in our Western culture, we have a very broad spectrum of musical expressions whose forms vary greatly one from another. Is beauty then in the ear of the listener? Is it the musical scales used, the notes played, the instruments used or the combination of, the relationship of the notes, the melodies, the harmonies? Any and all of these have something to do with producing the subjective experience of pleasure and beauty in the mind of the listener which raises the question once again: is beauty only a subjective experience in the mind, eye, or ear of the perceiver? If I remember correctly something I read long ago, a survey or study had discovered that certain shapes or forms found in the architecture of various cultures from various eras were commonly regarded as beautiful. There is here a hint that there may be qualities of the natural world or human design that represent beauty in a way that may be universally recognized. The beauty of certain mountains or mountain ranges may be another example or the colors of a spectacular sunset.

Can beauty also be said to be an aspect of the human mind in the sense that the recognition of beauty and the emotional experience it often evokes is an ability and tendency inherent in the mind? Could we say that this tendency is one of the finer, the "higher" characteristics of human consciousness, even one that may distinguish us from our animal relatives? Perhaps the ability and tendency to perceive and appreciate beauty is one of the things that makes us human. And perhaps beauty is an aspect of mind and creation because it is an aspect of the Creative Mind

or Power or Source from which everything arises, and was given
us in our creation. I leave these questions to you to decide.

> The power of mind to decide
> Carries within it the seeds of freedom.
> The rules by which we live
> Are given, predetermined, fixed.
> The law of gravity was not
> Decided in a teleconference.
> Natural laws were not voted
> Into existence. The law of karma,
> That every action has a consequence
> Determined by the nature of the act,
> Cannot be evaded or escaped.
> What you do unto others
> You are also doing unto yourself.
> This the law that assures
> Perfect justice accompanies all actions.
> The results of actions may not be
> Immediate, but they will come.
> What you give to another
> Is also being given to yourself.
> When you withhold love and kindness
> From your neighbor, you are also
> Being so deprived. The original law:
> Love thy neighbor as thyself
> Because your neighbor is yourself.
> Life is a Unity of Consciousness
> And Being. This fact can be denied
> But cannot be escaped.

> Freedom begins in the recognition
> Of the laws under which we live.
> The physical laws that are obvious

And the higher laws that are easier
To deny and overlook.
The body will always be
Limited, tied to the earth
Separate from other bodies
Subject to change and dissolution.
The Reality of Mind is where freedom awaits.
You need not struggle to create
Circumstances and conditions of life
In which you believe freedom
Will find you. It is not there
In the world of appearances,
Of constant change and uncertainty.
A freedom dependent upon
The shifting sands of life
Here one day, gone the next
Is but the appearance of freedom
Like a mirage in the desert
Seen from afar that disappears
The nearer you approach.
Real freedom arises from within
And characterizes the experience
Of one who has gone beyond
The temporary limitations of physicality
To experience the undying Essence
At the core of existence.
Neither struggle nor doing
Are required to reach it.
Undoing and surrender are
The way you become available
To the freedom that awaits
Only your recognition and acceptance.

To reach the freedom within,

The obstacles that clutter
And cloud the mind must
Be looked upon in full awareness
Must be recognized as what they are.
Fear is the great crippler
Of the human mind.
Where ignorance rules, where fear dominates,
Love is absent and freedom
Will not be found.
The absence of fear is Love.
Where love is, there is freedom also.
Love without freedom
Freedom without love is impossible.
When the mind is free to love
Suffering will come to an end.
Life awaits only your decision to be free.

Why does Love not characterize our actions and our lives? Not that it is entirely absent yet our human love is so often partial, relative. We love others for what they are to us, for what we get from them. In this there is always the element of exchange, as if love is a kind of emotional, even economic transaction in which it is not freely given but is dependent on what we can get, extract from each other. Often our love relationships involve a mutual dependence in which the continuation of our love depends on satisfying each other's "needs," including the sexual. This is not love, it is infatuation and desire. These are a part of human life, this cannot be denied, and are commonly confused with love due to the strong emotions involved both positive and negative. Where strong emotions and mutual dependence are involved, not infrequently there may be an emotional fluctuation commonly described as love/hate. One day love will seem to dominate, the next day anger or rage depending on circumstances or behavior. Love does not turn into hate or coexist with it in a back and forth dynamic.

In general human culture, certainly in the visual entertainment media and likewise in advertising, love seems to be most commonly associated with romance, with the delicate sexual and emotional dance between two people that often, at least in the past, can lead to marriage and children. Love is hopefully a part of this but it is limited and exclusive; limited to one's partner and family and excluding others with the exception of close friends. Love under any circumstances or conditions is to be welcomed whether partial and exclusionary or not, yet what is needed in our society and all others, particularly at this time of great division and conflict between peoples, nations, and within society itself, is the Love that is all inclusive and is based on forgiveness and tolerance.

Jesus said in response to his disciples' questions about loving others that anyone can love those that love you, even the publicans do that (the publicans were the tax collectors of those times, were known for their greed and dishonesty, and were generally despised by the people of Israel). Jesus taught his disciples that they were to love their enemies, to pray for and do good to those that hated and persecuted them. To be kind to all and offer forgiveness to all, even to those who have hurt us, without any conditions, seems to be the most difficult thing for us to do as human beings judging by the history of the human race, even the history of Christian nations. Is there any better guide to human behavior, for our interactions with each other no matter what level or circumstance; is any other way of acting liable to bring peace and harmony between people and nations? We have tried every other approach, all of which are based on fear, defensiveness, and selfishness; all our attempts have simply continued the parade of conflict, separation and disharmony that characterizes so much of human life.

The kindness and benevolence that are also present in our society on many levels are responsible for holding our civilization together up to the present. In the light of the divisions that have arisen on so many levels, the pressures that are building, the unsustainability of our present way of life, and the instability of civilization on a global scale, I would say it's time now to step it up, to commit to loving and forgiving each other in a way that has seldom been practiced before on a large scale. I am speaking here to each and every one of us, not society as a whole. When we look at the world scene or the situation in our nation, the question arises as to what can any individual do at this critical time?

The best thing we can do, perhaps the only thing we can do, is to change our minds and behavior, to dedicate our lives to Love, kindness, and forgiveness at all times, in all situations, in all places. Let all of our actions arise from this dedication and commitment. Let this be our base, our foundation; let all thoughts, actions, and words proceed from Love. In each and every moment of our lives, no matter what we are doing, we can be part of the solution to fear, hatred and conflict; Love is the solution and we can be that Love, or we can be part of the problem, caught in fear and acting it out one way or another.

The Love of God
Is all there is,
Pervading all time and space
Yet beyond all limitation.
Surrounded by that Love,
Separated by unawareness
The ignorance of selffullness
Obscures the sun with dark
Heavy clouds of forgetfulness.
Grace is everywhere offered
It cannot enter where
Refusal and rejection rise
To bar the door.

The gifts of God are
Freely given to all
Who would receive them
And offered to those who would not.

Grace cannot enter a mind
That values attack and lives
In fear of God and Love.
Your Creator does not force
Himself upon you, does not
Violate the gift of free will
You were given at the moment
Of creation. Always you decide
On what enters your life
What occupies your mind.
Choose suffering, it will
Be given you, choose redemption
It will accompany you
On your journey through the
Darkness of separation. Always
You decide and always you
Receive the consequences of what
Has been chosen. Free will
Must be used wisely if
You would transcend suffering.
Choices appear to be many
There are only two, only two.
Truth and illusion are always
The inner content of what
Faces you and demands decision.
Of these two, only one
Is real. Choose illusion
And you will suffer.
Choose Truth and It

Will guide you home.
The journey down the
Dusty roads of space/time
Is a process of learning
What is Truth, what is illusion
And the difference between them.
No matter the many forms in which
Choice appears, the only thing
You ever do is choose the
Content of Truth or illusion
And their consequences.

Pilgrimage to the place of the wise is to find escape
from the flame of separation.
Jalaluddin Rumi

Chapter 8

The Universal

The day was warm, an occasional gentle breeze rustling the leaves of the trees that still wore their summer green though here and there the bright yellow of autumn was beginning to appear. A softness, a gentle contentment, seemed to permeate the forest and the meadows scattered throughout; you could feel it and drink it in. It soothed the heart and left the mind quiet and at rest. Very few people were about so I had the narrow trail mostly to myself. It wound its way through forest and the meadows whose tall plants had already turned brown after several months without rain. It was not a drab brown, but a golden brown that was pleasing to the eye. Walking in silence, the blissful Presence that was both within and without absorbed my attention until I stopped, unable to go any farther. Resting in pure Being, in Spirit, all things around me became part of me, resting in my heart as though they were arising within it.

There is a Source of all existence from which, in which, all arises and has its Being. Call It what you will; God, Spirit, Allah, Brahman, Creator, all life and intelligence is part of That without Which nothing is. The schisms between religions and spiritual belief systems have nothing to do with the Source. Differing interpretations, symbols, methods of worship and practice need not create conflictual divisions. Different peoples require different sets of symbols, practices, and interpretations that speak to them and bring them into communion with the Source. In this as in so many other ways, the various groupings of humanity have found their own unique approaches and ways of relating to the Sacred.

The experiences of the spiritual, the sacred dimension of existence, have a universal character. The spiritual literature of the authentic religions and spiritual traditions demonstrate and describe a fundamental commonality in the experiences of many individuals belonging to different religions and spiritual traditions from ancient times until our present era. Neither time nor space seem to affect this universality of sacred experience. The problem of religious conflict does not arise there. Gandhi's famous dictum, "God has no religion," expresses well this fundamental truth: God is one, religions are many.

The experience is One but the interpretations are many. Unfortunately what can happen, and seems to have often happened when someone belonging to a particular religion has authentic and profound spiritual experience, is that the experience is taken as "proof" or evidence of the rightness of that religion and all its dogma though much of the dogma is simply a matter of belief, not of experience. And the fact that someone of another religious tradition has had the same or very similar experiences is overlooked, ignored, or denied simply on the basis of belief, belief that has very little if anything to do with experience. Somehow the other guy's experience does not validate his religion. This attitude is further strengthened by the general ignorance of other religions that commonly prevails among believers of any one religion. Adding to the already complicated situation is the egoic tendency, the need to be right, and in so doing to make the others wrong. As religion is most fundamentally a belief system about the nature of reality and how we should live, it is heavily defended, adding another very emotional element to the mix, making clear thinking even more difficult and less likely.

God is One, always, everywhere
No change anytime, anywhere.
What is beyond space and time
Cannot be touched by the
Fleeting whims of fancy

And belief. Better not to stop
With belief, with images of That
Which cannot be captured by words.
The Creative Source of all that is
Is ever present, waiting
For you to care, to look up
From what you are doing
And discover the beauty
That surrounds you.

The Call goes out everywhere
At all times, unceasing.
It cannot be heard by
The mind filled with greed and desire.
Confusion fills the mind captured by its
Visions of glitter and gold.
The mind cannot hold idols it would worship
And the vision of the One.
Mind can serve one purpose
One master, there is no room
No place, for two.
To think otherwise is
To be lost in delusion.
We serve God or mammon
Love or fear, Truth or illusion.
Learn to live from that
Which is highest in you.
Call it Soul or Spirit or Self.
To follow what is temporary,
Passing, is to sever your
Connection with the Source that gives
You life. Choose against life
Death will be your reward.

The evidence of Spirit
Is all around you.
The Wholeness of Intelligence
And Life, the love in the eyes
Of your brothers and sisters,
The compassion and kindness
In your heart, tell you a story
Of a deeper life and purpose
Than the surface of things.
The depths of Life cannot be
Measured by the superficial
Mind of pleasure and forgetfulness.
Shallow perception and experience
See only the obvious, never
The meaning and purpose
That infuse existence and
Give it life.

What is it to be loved by God? What does that mean actually? Are there tangible benefits that result from being the recipient of God's love? Before one can recognize benefit, one has to accept That which gives the benefit. This seems to be obviously true. The Love of God is not simply offered to all, It is given to all yet is not accepted by all. In our creation, we were given all of the gifts of God as a part of what we are. This will never change. The mind that was created by God to be One with Him, an extension of His Love, has forgotten its Source and its true Being. In the state of separation from Truth, Love is denied and reduced to distorted versions of Itself. What is all encompassing and non-exclusionary by its very nature, is expressed through relationships that exclude all others. Remembering God and opening ourselves to feel, to receive the Love He would give, is necessary to receive. To forget or ignore or deny the existence of That in Which we live and move and have our Being, is to successfully refuse Love; you cannot receive what is not valued and accepted.

In Truth, we are surrounded and sustained by the Love of God. Like fish we are swimming in an ocean, though not of water, an ocean of Love. And like fish who don't see the water they live in, we cannot see the Ocean in which we live. Love, like spirit, cannot be seen by the body's eyes, but through the mind and heart It can be perceived, felt, and directly experienced. Though intangible to the physical senses, the gifts of Spirit can be perceived, directly sensed by consciousness itself for consciousness is an attribute of Spirit, not of matter, though it functions through physical instruments such as the brain and nervous system.

"By their fruits you shall know them." Though not visible, the fruits, the effects of Love, are everywhere present in human life. The kindness of strangers, the many acts of goodwill and helpfulness that occur every day in the lives of many: all are expressions of Love in action. Love is not absent in this world. Though often denied, It is still present in muted form; without Love would life be a joyless and brutal existence.

When night falls across the land
And our footsteps grow silent.
Sleep embraces town and country,
The empty lanes and roads
Fill with shadows and the
Scurrying of small creatures.

The many who once
Roamed forest and meadow
Have not gone, they watch us still.
Listen to the sounds
Of flowing waters, you will hear
The quiet voices that once

Were everywhere, on the hills
In the valleys and along
The great rivers. What will
We say to those who knew
The ancient forests we cut down?
How to explain the
Poisoning of the waters
And where the life that shared
This land with us has gone?

We live not for today
But tomorrow. Always must
We have more, more!
Never is there enough to fill
The great emptiness where our
Soul used to be. We have
Sold our soul for thirty
Pieces of silver. There is
Nothing left to do but take
Our place upon the cross
We have built in place
Of the life that used to be.

Redemption, freely given
Waits for all. No turning back,
The past is dead, let it lie
Among the fallen trees that once
Lined the roads we must travel.
Look not behind or ahead
But move steadily forward.
Where we walk is empty space.
Leave no footprints, you do not
Need them on this journey.
We are returning to where

We have always been.

Philosophy used to be defined and understood as the love and pursuit of wisdom. Down through the ages there have been many who have made an attempt in good faith to arrive at reasonable answers to the fundamental question or questions of existence. This is true of the cultures of East and West, both of which have produced a large body of what could be called philosophy.

What passes for philosophy in the modern era seems no longer to be the love of wisdom but rather the love of empty and useless intellectualizing. This may get you tenure and a teaching position somewhere in academia as well as the admiration of many like yourself, but does it bring you closer to the great mystery of which you are part or give your life meaning? The mind can be kept busy with constant verbalization and other activity. It can worship itself and its own arrogance but never will it find real meaning or happiness thereby. Never will the reduction of the miracle of life to empty concepts and unproven theories treated as fact result in anything but bitter fruit, no matter how many honors you may attain or receive.

The purpose of the intellect is to reason, to weigh and measure, to help bring about understanding. If presented with a problem needing solution or an issue needing understanding, the intellect can be applied to reach a necessary conclusion. In that case, the facts or relevant factors presented to the intellect for it to consider are of great importance for the final result. Here the "garbage in, garbage out" principle applies. The exclusion of possibly relevant information from consideration can play a major role regarding the validity or non-validity of conclusions that may be reached. In any case where the intellect is applied to attain a particular result be it understanding, a conclusion, or a solution, the final result depends not only on the power of the intellect, of the reasoning, thinking process, but on the information, the so-called facts relevant to the issue that are included and those which are excluded. Obviously the choice of material used in the process of thinking and considering is essential for the final result. Choice is vitally important to the whole process, and choices are heavily influenced by preexistent factors such as bias, value judgments, and previous experience or the lack of it. These factors predate the application of intellect to a particular event or situation in time.

When you look at a particular issue from the public domain, an issue that is argued strongly from multiple viewpoints, with diligent examination you can usually find more than one carefully reasoned argument. A process of careful reasoning leading to a plausible conclusion has been apparently employed despite the very different conclusions that have been reached for each viewpoint. Clearly the differing conclusions arrived at, the opposing opinions, are not due simply to the application of the intellect. They are the result of the facts used, the facts ignored, and usually certain value judgments, all of which vary from one side to another. What is important in this process is not so much the intellect itself; the intellect is, after all, just a tool though in some circles that seems to be forgotten. What often plays the decisive role is the choice of facts to use and not use, and the underlying values of the participants that influence this choice.

After observing this obvious dynamic which plays out everywhere in human life including the realm of science, it seems to me one can draw two very clear conclusions: firstly, that the use of the intellect is virtually never uninfluenced by bias and a priori assumptions, and secondly, it is the biases good or bad, true or false, and the values and belief systems of individuals that more than anything influence conclusions supposedly reached by the application of reason. Reason and intellect are used more as a sort of after the fact exercise to justify or prove what is believed to be true. This assertion is actually applicable to our belief systems as a whole as well as to any one opinion or belief about anything. Arthur C. Clarke, the famous science fiction writer of the twentieth century, was known to have said: "For every expert there is an equal and opposite expert." Again, assuming that at least certain major facts are generally known and considered, there is nonetheless in virtually all areas of human life and thought fundamental disagreements on just about everything. And the reason, as has been previously stated and is probably pretty obvious to common sense, is the different biases, the individual opinions we hold regarding good or bad, important or unimportant, valuable or not valuable. In short, the lack of a consensus on what to do or what is true in relation to human life is because of the lack of consensus on what we value and do not value. Another way to say this: there is a lack of recognition of a common purpose to which we all subscribe.

The lack of common purpose, this difference on such a basic level, cannot be fully overcome in our social and political life as a society. The best we can do is work towards compromise which allows society to function going forward. That is in effect the purpose of Democracy: to provide a government framework that represents the diverse elements of the population and whose functionaries, the elected representatives, work together to provide legislation that supports the interests of the greatest number of citizens. This requires compromise to bridge the gap between competing factions, compromise in which some gain and some loss over time is inevitable and unavoidable for virtually all members of society. That this is grudgingly accepted, if at all, goes without saying. Yet without this acceptance, when anger turns into extremism and a tendency to refuse necessary compromises that reach all the way up to the elected representatives themselves, effective, fair, and mature governance becomes very difficult and is itself compromised. The behavior of some of our public officials today can only be described as childish. Despite their education, intelligence, and the responsibility they carry, some are acting like vengeful adolescents and this is shameful to say the least.

There is a life we all share
No matter liberal or conservative
Atheist, agnostic or believer;
We eat every day
Go to work, come home
Play, sleep, take care of
Our families. All have those
They love and support.
We share the sunlight
And the dark night,
The wind blows and the rain
Falls on us all.
Each deserves food, a roof overhead
Love, and meaningful work,
Help when they are sick
And cooperation in the
Interest of the whole.
No man is an island
No woman either or child
None can make a life alone.
We all need the help
The work, the goodwill
Of our fellow citizens.
A house divided cannot stand.
A society isolated each from
Their neighbors, without common
Purpose, cannot withstand the
Changes that are coming.
The four horsemen are on the gallop
Across the face of the earth
Bringing death and destruction.
United we must stand together
Or we will all fall separately.

What is it that you like to do? Not just what amuses you or gives you pleasure or provides a pleasant distraction from the worries of life, but something you like to do for its own sake, something that feels good and gives you a sense of satisfaction or fulfillment. There are many things we can do that may amuse us, may keep our attention focused on one activity or another for at least a little while. We seek stimulation and entertainment in many different ways, yet at the end of all this activity a feeling of emptiness remains.

The surface details of life, so much of what we think, do, or say, is actually very unimportant in light of the purpose, the meaning of our existence. Notwithstanding the overwhelming and constant assault on your attention by economic mechanisms such as advertising among others that try twenty-four/seven to convince you happiness and fulfillment depend on how much material wealth you accumulate, how many different forms of pleasure you indulge in, and how many new toys you own and fads you pursue: does a life reduced to these banalities seem meaningful to you? Is such a life, being manipulated by the carrot on a stick held before your nose as if you were a donkey, blinded by the lure of a constantly changing and supposedly better tomorrow: is such a life truly worth living? Is the identity of a consumer, one whose activity and value are determined by the marketplace, sufficient?

These are questions I hope everyone will eventually ponder and answer. The answer you give yourself will tell you a lot about where you are in your life and where you are going. The answer, whether yes or no, is a step forward if honestly given. Real progress, in the sense of discovery of and commitment to the deeper meaning and purpose of life, must begin with self-honesty, which continues to be increasingly important as we journey towards final understanding and the realization of Truth. Real and consistent, even relentless self-honesty is a necessity if you would lead a life of authentic insight, meaning and purpose.

A state of deep peace, "the peace of God," cannot be attained unless the mind becomes aware of all the obstacles to peace that live in its depths and influence its responses. Obstructions must be observed and recognized; a real willingness to look at everything in our mind, the "bad" as well as the "good," and measure them by a higher standard is necessary. What falls short must be steadily relinquished, a process that requires abundant willingness, honesty, self-awareness, and perseverance over time.

What if you say no
To everything that surrounds you?
Lay it down, put it aside,
Leave it behind even for a
Moment of time. Stand alone
Naked before life, before Truth.
Let the mind empty itself
Of all thoughts, all it knows
And does not know, all feelings
And moods, all opinions about
Anything. Remind yourself,
"I know nothing." Say it
Like you mean it. Stand
Alone in the Light, the awareness
Of pure Being. Not this
Not that, just Being Itself
Beyond labels, beyond names,
Identity-less, egoless, neither I-ness
Nor other-ness. Stand beyond
All concepts, beliefs, doubts.
Unafraid, unattached to what
Has been, to what might be.
Let Truth Itself devastate
Whatever sense of identity

Remains. Dissolve into the great Silence
And Emptiness at the core of Being.
No resistance, surrender to That
Which is highest of all,
The Source of all, the Intelligence
And power immeasurable
From which all arises.

Let not the past confine
You to what is over and gone
Or let idle fantasies and
Future dreams dim the mind
While the present passes you by.
The blindness that hobbles
The mind is correctable.
Blindness is learned. It
Rests on choice and repetition.
Choose again and again
To see what waits for
Recognition. It has not left
You alone and helpless.
Within and without, all around
Is a Light which can be seen
With open eyes and mind.
The choice of blindness
Has left you unable to see
That by Which you live.
Choose again!

To the west the white clouds have taken on the golden hue of the sunset; to the south where the light is blocked by the long ridges of the low mountains, the clouds are a leaden gray. Overhead they spread lazily across the sky, sometimes gray, sometimes gold, and the light blue of the sky is fading as the day comes to an end. A living beauty, simple but profound, is the sky at sunset. All of nature is like that; unpretentious, simple and direct, forest and mountain, desert and seashore, the sandy reaches of the high plateaus and the deep canyons with their depths muffled in shadow. A natural beauty, always changing through the seasons as the play of light and weather do their part to add variety, to express the different moods of Mother Earth. She supports us all, feeds us all. How many of us are grateful?

Gratitude brings love and appreciation as surely as fear leads to anger and sadness. It is good to be grateful, grateful to our Mother Earth for her gifts, grateful to our fellow human beings for their help. Life for us is a cooperative venture requiring many to play their parts well, whatever they may be, for human society to function. Each deserves the gratitude of us all. All the creatures who share the earth with us, who share life with us, have a place in the richness and depth of existence. We are surrounded by beauty and mystery; to forget this fact and live in a state of distraction and forgetfulness, with downcast eyes and weary steps, is to never have truly lived. You are not a stagnant, backwater pool, muddy, surrounded by shadows. You are the living waters of a swiftly moving stream, clear and transparent, reflecting the bright sunlight above, dancing your way through mountains and across the plains on your happy journey back to the sea. The great Ocean, the source of life-giving waters, awaits your return as if you had never left. All streams, all rivers return to the sea, their origin and Source. Life does not and will not cease ever.

What does life mean to you? Is your existence something unquestioned, unexamined, just a brute fact of experience, of action and reaction, of suffering and joy, of attraction and aversion? Is there a place in your mind where you are aware of what you think and why? Are you aware of your feelings, of where they come from, when they arise, and why? Do you respond gracefully to the changes and difficulties of life or are you caught in a cycle of simply reacting to them, being driven and controlled by the circumstances around you? Our response to what happens to us is the determiner of how we live. Assume the victim role, merely react to life's conditions without reflection or self-understanding, and your life will be directionless like a sailboat driven in whatever direction the wind seems to blow. Take responsibility for your emotions and reactions, become familiar with how your mind works, and you will have the possibility to respond rather than react and chart your own course among the changes and conditions of your life. The power of decision is your own; use it wisely, being aware of your own mind and how it works, of your strengths and weaknesses, and you will have the opportunity to make positive choices, ones that will truly benefit yourself and others.

When you consider human life honestly, look through the lens of history, look at the present situation and condition, and observe the human mind with its many contradictions, inconsistencies, and its good qualities, clearly there are good and positive aspects that make life worth living. Yet there is something else also, something that cannot be denied. One can see, can sense a kind of sadness, an overlay that is inherent in life itself, unavoidably inherent in the human condition, always present, if not here today, then possibly tomorrow. I believe this is what Thoreau was referring to in his famous statement about the human condition mentioned elsewhere in these pages. The "quiet desperation" he referred to is a state of mind dominated by an unacknowledged sadness, and a constant activity whose purpose is to keep sadness at bay by directing focus and attention elsewhere.

From where or what does this sense of sadness arise? The fact that death waits for us all is the root which gives birth to all negative emotions that plague the human mind. Somewhere in the journey from childhood to adulthood the fact of death becomes part of awareness though often muted and kept at bay. Death is seldom talked about or discussed in our Western culture; there is a kind of taboo in effect, a taboo that is seldom violated. Almost like the game very young children play when they close their eyes and pretend that something isn't there because they no longer see it. There is no acknowledgement of death in Disneyland; it's bad for business. It's difficult to convince ourselves that all the objects of desire we so assiduously accumulate to bring us happiness are really that valuable if we admit to ourselves we will only possess them for a little while until death snatches them from our grasp. To maintain the fictions on which modern life is based, the temporality, the temporariness of bodily life and all the goals, honors, and achievements we may attain must be forgotten. You can't enjoy the party if you realize that death is the designated driver; maybe not tonight, maybe not tomorrow, but sooner or later your number will come up and meanwhile the meter is running and you know that someday the bill will come due.

The fact of death must be thoroughly ignored, forgotten even, just to get on with our life. At the very least, it must be kept in the background, somewhere on the periphery of consciousness, barely acknowledged and never discussed. Yet what lives in our mind, no matter whether it is denied and delegated to the subconscious, will nevertheless have its effect. Death casts a heavy shadow across our lives, one that can be ignored when the sun is brightly shining though it never goes away. Hence the underlying current of sadness that runs through all life.

Is it possible to live from a mood of joy, from a recognition of life as it really is in all its depth, richness, and meaning, and from an awareness of the role played by death? For the human mind, death is the end of everything, the final extinction of all our hopes and aspirations, the end of our consciousness and existence itself. It stands before us, a great abyss, dark and empty into which we must descend, leaving all life, all memory, and everyone we love behind. The ultimate loneliness of death is inescapable; no one can die your death but you, nobody can accompany you as you leave this world behind and enter that long dark tunnel. If death is the end of everything we love, then is real happiness impossible to achieve. If, no matter how glorious our life, in the end is everything reduced to dust and ashes, then is life ultimately meaningless.

Fortunately, despite many appearances to the contrary, that is not the case; life is not meaningless unless you choose to reduce it to those terms. Meaning is intrinsic to Life, Being, Consciousness. Meaning does not depend on human opinion, bias for or against, acceptance or denial. Universal meaning is inherent in self-awareness, independent of whether any particular mind realizes that or not. Nothing as important as meaning has been left captive to the whims of human ego. The meaning and purpose of life are there for each and every one of us to discover and accept. We can live in denial of this fact and descend into the despair of mindless nihilism, or invent our own meaning that grows out of the need for pleasure and stimulation, or from the ambition to amass wealth, attain status or power. Never will our inventions or imagination free us from the fear of death that haunts the human mind. Never will the haunting specter of death's grim smile fail to gaze mockingly on all our accomplishments, waiting for that inevitable moment when we collapse and lay prostrate amidst the rubble of our life's end.

The good news is that death, while an undeniable part of our experience of life, is not the end but rather a transition from one state of consciousness to another, from one realm of experience to another. As such, even if an unpleasant event as it often seems to be, if one has a real understanding of its significance, not just mental but a deeper, more experiential understanding, then is the passage through death a very different experience. To recognize that your life in its entirety is not bound by the little interval between the parentheses of birth and death; that this life is a small part of something much greater, is essential. With

that realization, is the possibility yours to free yourself from
the crippling fear of death and begin the journey towards the
recovery of your Wholeness and freedom.

Life or death, which will you choose?
Lead a life that is
A living death, or die
Into new life?
Not simply an experience,
Death is a state of mind
An attitude, and orientation towards life
And all that surrounds you.
To join, to share, to give
Is life itself, its movement
And its meaning. To fear,
To isolate, to separate and
Defend is to choose death
While alive. The great irony:
Choose life as it is
Choose well, and become deathless.
Choose death while alive
And become lifeless.
Any moment is the time
Of your living or the time
Of your dying. Die many
Deaths or live many lives.
Two choices in which
Everything is included.

* * *

What else to do
While you walk the earth?
Serve and help all who come.

Let none pass by without
Your smile to light their way.
The journey seems long and hard
Bereft of hope sometimes
The end uncertain.
Hold each other's hand
Let the strong hold up
Those who falter. The weak
Shall become strong, the last
Shall be first. The race is won
By those who finish.
Those who reach the top
Of the mountain all have
The same view. Names mean
Nothing on the summit.
To arrive, you must leave
The ego at the bottom.

From the valleys below
Come the sounds of conflict,
The screams of the wounded
The moans of the dying.
From the battlefield
Nothing can be done.
Rise above the struggle
On wings of Love. Let compassion
Ease the suffering of fear and hate.
Look upon all with forgiveness
Give what you would receive.
See the Light hidden in everyone,
Remember the Truth that is
Concealed by the images of separation.
Let the Truth in you join
The Truth in your brothers

And become One, only One.

Love is that which binds us together, the invisible glue that holds the many different elements and factions of a society in meaningful and cooperative relationship. Without a sense of togetherness – we are all in this together – there is no recognition of mutual benefit to underpin the acceptance and tolerance required for any society to be functional and capable of providing a meaningful degree of well-being to most of its members. An attitude of goodwill towards others in general, no matter how grudgingly given at times, is the basis of the trust that supports our cooperative endeavors. Wherever trust and goodwill are absent is cooperation impossible to achieve.

The beauty of each day is something to be discovered within the conditions and circumstances all around you. Each day and every moment holds within it hell or heaven. When you choose Love, you are choosing to be happy and extending that happiness to the world around you. By Love, I am not referring to emotional or sexual infatuation or obsession. Love in everyday life expresses as a feeling of goodwill, kindness, and helpfulness to others. Love is patient and avoids negative judgments and unnecessary criticisms; is tolerant and allows others the freedom to be as they are without trying to use or manipulate them. Love does not envy others or covet their possessions and successes, but rather rejoices in their good fortune. It does not compare or rank others based on any external criteria. Through the eyes of Love are all seen as what they are: children of the One Creator and equally beloved. The Essence of all is One and in that are all equal. None stands higher or lower in the Creator's sight. In time, in this world, there are many differences among us; this cannot be denied. In expression, in the world of form and separation, we are different in many ways: appearance, talents, abilities, behavior etc. In Truth, in our core, our Essence, each is an equal expression of the One Creator.

In each of us the one Love that embraces all waits for discovery and expression that It may set us free and work through us to extend this freedom to others. At this time in our history, this terrible time of genocide, of increasing hatred, division, and conflict, there is nothing the world needs more than love and forgiveness among peoples, among individuals, among those of different creeds, religions, nations, races, ethnicities. This may seem naïve, impractical, incapable of resolving the great problems we face and yet tension and conflict are always the result of the absence of Love, forgiveness, and tolerance, their place being occupied by fear, hatred, and separation. I speak here to myself and to the individuals who share the planet with me and each other. I do not say our problems will be resolved but we must try each and every one of us to be part of the solution or we will continue to be part of the problem. What can ever be done by any of us but to bring our own lives into alignment with higher law, the Law of Love? "Do unto others as you would have them do unto you." Give others what you would yourself receive. The law of karma assures us that the consequences of our words and actions will return to us. We cannot injure another without injuring ourselves. Likewise, we cannot love another, do good, give help, without that love, that good, returning to bless us as well.

In light of the higher laws, it is obvious the best way, the only sane way to live is to be Love. This has been taught in one variation or another by the saints, sages, the awakened ones of all spiritual traditions for thousands of years. Perhaps it's time to apply this understanding, to learn to live by the higher laws, by the law of Love before it's too late. Each of us must choose how we would live. In that choice lies the future of our civilization, our planet, and all who live upon it.

When Love comes calling
What will you do?

Our brothers, naked and hungry
Walk the streets of our cities.
Love looks through their sad eyes
Speaks through their trembling voices
Asks our forgiveness for what
We have done. Mother Earth
Who feeds us all, clothes us
Lies beneath our careless feet
Unloved, unthanked.
She wishes only to bless
To give what is needed
For life and love.

The creatures of forest,
Mountain and desert, always
At the mercy of human
Indifference ask nothing of us.
Do they deserve to live too?
Our songbird friends no longer sing
Like before. Many are gone.
Carelessness, unrestrained development
Have stilled their many voices.
Mornings are silent now
No happiness greets the day.

When is there joy in the land?
Who greets the sunrise with
Open arms and a glad heart?
If not you, then who?
Who will defend the earth
That nourishes our bodies
And sustains our souls?
If not you, then who?
My world, your world, our world,

All the same world. Who knows
What will happen and when?
The day is given you
To spend in a worthy manner.
Worthy means having worth or value.
Look at your activities.
Is there benefit for you or others?
Benefit in stuffing yourself
With food, in drugging the
Body and the mind? Benefit
In fantasies, playing with new toys,
Seeking escape and stimulation
Chasing the phantom of happiness?
To look for it where it
Is not is never to find it.

Fill your days with concern
For others and happiness
Will find you and make your
Heart its home. Love and
Be helpful whenever you can.
Kindness and forgiveness in all
Relationships help to make
The world a better place.
Do your part and you will
Be better too. All are
Called at this critical time.
Each has a part to play
That is yours alone. Help dispel
The darkness with the light
Of your love.

The goodwill of many
Is needed to heal the earth

And the heart of humanity.
To ease the pain of many and
The misery of fear and loss.
You cannot turn away, close your eyes
There is no place to hide.
We are all part of these changing times.
Do not let yourself and your brothers
And sisters suffer alone. Hear
Their cries, offer the compassion
Of your heart and the helpfulness
Of your thoughts and actions.
We need the best from each other
Not business as usual.
The choice is yours though
There is no choice.

The awakening to Truth is the disappearance of the ego,
the sense of a separate self.
From the Christ Mind, Book II

Chapter 9

Perhaps It's Time

An active love and concern, a helpfulness not limited to friends and family; the great teachers of history have tried to set our feet on this path. It's time to learn what they tried to teach us. In times of war or great tragedy, it is the heroism of many that saves the day, that helps us get through. Love is the source of our heroism and self-sacrifice. From love for one another we act, even to the point of risking or losing our own lives. "Greater love hath no man than this, that he lay down his life for his friends." These words of Jesus Christ have rung true down through the ages. Again and again have so-called ordinary men and women accomplished great things in the midst of great upheaval and horrific circumstances. This potential to rise to the occasion when called to do so lives in each and every one of us. Selfless acts of love and service become common when circumstances require it. Less common yet always present are the lives of heroic dedication to the service of others, to the highest good as exemplified by the saints, great reformers, and leaders. There is no shortage of proof of the greatness of human beings, of the potential that lives in the heart and soul of each and every one of us.

Little acts of love and heroism are no less important than the great sacrifices of some; these expressions of helpfulness and kindness happen all around us every day. Without an attitude of goodwill toward each other, human society becomes very bleak. "No man is an island," this is true of all whether male or female. Humans are not meant to live alone and isolated. From a tribe in the tropical rainforest to rural villages to megalopolises, cooperative living seems to be the way we are meant to live. It is ironic that in modern cities, with their high population densities, the opposite is occurring. Isolation seems to be increasing and direct communication between individuals is being replaced by indirect means such as e-mails, texting etc. Never have there been so many different ways to communicate and yet so little direct communication between individuals. If this trend continues, who knows where it will lead?

When help is needed, help is given if the willingness to receive is there. A spiritual provision is potentially available to all but this potential must be realized, i.e. the mind must make the commitment to healing itself of anger, fear, and judgment, and begin the necessary process of surrender to and alignment with the Higher Power, with Love. As long as the choice is made to go one's own way, to rely on one's self alone, no room is given to the possibility of receiving help which thus negates the ability to receive it. "Ask and you will be given," means you must be open to receiving help and request it. And the mind must be willing to be healed of negativity and willing to take serious steps in that direction.

To not seek and receive the help so freely offered and given is a great loss of tragic proportions. Life has many twists and turns, unforeseen events; it can be very trying even in our wealthy and comfortable society. There are none that could not benefit from the perspective of Higher Intelligence. To receive, however, one has to relinquish all need to control outcomes and learn to trust. When help is received, it may not be what was hoped for or expected, likewise with the outcome, but the final result will be in one's best (highest) interest and in the best interest of all others who may be affected.

Although there appears to be an almost infinite number of ways to live, especially in free and democratic pluralistic societies such as ours, in actuality, only two possibilities exist. In the sense of the outer life, the physical details, actions etc., the life of appearances, indeed there are many different forms and apparent directions life can take that are determined by many factors both external and internal. However, as noted elsewhere in these pages, individual life takes place fundamentally in consciousness. Without consciousness, there is no experience, no human life. A primary fact of existence is this inner life where we experience what occurs to us and around us as well as our interpretations of and reactions to these happenings. Motivations, judgments, evaluations, thoughts and feelings, all take place within, and are the actual basis of our lives. In a very basic sense then, all life can be described as occurring in an outer and/or an inner sense. All experience belongs to one or the other of these two movements in consciousness.

The inner content of consciousness is what we really are; it's where we really live. Inner content is dominated by love, by positivity, or by fear and negativity. Most of us fluctuate back and forth between the two extremes, animating first the positive inner content of consciousness, then shifting to the negative or vice versa. This movement goes on throughout the day and throughout our lives. Some days may be more positive, others more negative; this dynamic varies greatly from person to person with different ratios of positive to negative generally characteristic of each individual mind. The ratios themselves undergo regular change which tends to take place within certain limits determined by individual outlook and perspective on life, values, the degree of self-awareness, and outer circumstances.

Back and forth like a kite
In the wind is the mind
Without self understanding.
Driven by circumstances
And crippled by ignorance
The mind is helpless.
Difficult indeed is life
Without a light to follow
That illuminates the darkness.

By itself, the mind stumbles
Along, unaware of what
Obstacles bar its way.
It cannot see what is there
Through the fog that surrounds it.

Whenever the light appears
The darkness is lifted if
Only for a little while.
Do not wait for the light
To find you. You can seek for it
Everywhere, you will find it
Within. The ego does not
Know of it nor can ego
Reach what lies far beyond it.
In the depths of mind
Below the constant activity
Of thought, of feelings, below
The noise of everyday life,
Waiting for you to go beyond
Yourself, the portal, the great
Silence at the heart of all.

Lose yourself in the Silence
You will not find yourself again.
Gone the need to be what you
Are not. Leave the world of sleep
Behind, step into the Light
That illuminates existence.
Carry Light wherever you go,
Learn to see it everywhere, in everyone.
Be guided in everything you do.

Be your own guide?

Follow the drives, impulses
And habits that dominate
Your mind? Repeat yourself
Over and over again.
Live through the past and miss
What is here and now.
Be as a boat tossed about
By the waves on the stormy
Seas of life.

The choice is yours
Always and everywhere.
You must choose the guide to follow.
The ego will take you
Nowhere and spend a long time
Getting there. Listen to the Guide
Who knows the way, Who knows you
As you are. Let Him help you
Decide on the questions of life.
Ask Him anything, He will
Provide the answer you need.
Not to worry, nothing to fear.
The only thing to lose is
The attachment to suffering.
What is valued by worldly
Mind is the cause of suffering.

The way is not easy
But leads to freedom and love.
The way of the world leads to death.
Choose life or death, Love or fear
Freedom or bondage, always
This you choose with every
Decision. Sooner or later

You must learn the difference
Between Truth and illusion.

Do you know the purpose of your life or does it even have a purpose? Do you move blindly from one event to another, avoiding, hiding from what threatens you whether within or without? A life of routine: eating, sleeping, drinking, getting "high," sexing, trying to lose yourself in activities, distract yourself with stimulation and entertainment? Being carried along by urges, impulses, attraction and aversion, all kinds of unconscious tendencies, will lead neither to happiness nor a state of inner peace not to mention freedom.

The condition of life of so many in our times is life without purpose or, as with some, living without even the idea of purpose. Swept along, shaped by the conditions around you, by societally determined factors and the accumulated cultural habits of centuries, conditioned by the consensus view of reality; where is there room for understanding, for thoughtful contemplation and meaningful creativity, for authentic living? Most of us live a kind of "hand me down" life, never having taken the time to step out beyond the parameters of life's possibilities that we were taught, even to the point of never thinking "outside the box" as the slogan goes. We are not meant to follow in the well-worn footsteps of worldly society, the ruts worn deep into the earth by the generations that preceded us. We need not water the earth with our tears or spill our blood needlessly in the meaningless conflicts that continually arise as expressions of the human need to hate and fear one another.

Perhaps it's time to refuse to accept and believe what is so constantly asserted and displayed in public life, in the media, even in our relationships with each other. We are surrounded by a vast realm of nonsense masquerading as knowledge or truth. This nonsense takes many forms and appears in every realm of human endeavor. We cannot expect what is nonsense to admit its meaninglessness to us, or those who believe and defend it, to lift the veil and reveal the nothingness behind it. Each of us is responsible for our life in all its particulars: our thoughts, feelings, beliefs, words and actions, and the consequences thereof. Much of what is carried in our minds is the result of conditioning, of the influence of education, training, external circumstances, opinions of friends and family, and the cultural beliefs of the society in which we live. Some of what is learned is true or useful and deserves to be kept; much of it is nonsense or distortion and needs to be carefully examined and reconsidered. The learning process through childhood and adolescence is to a great extent unconscious and automatic. In that sense, it could be described as "accidental." There are those, perhaps many, who never become aware of this fact or question it or go beyond it.

To live a truly human life, to explore the potential carried within as well as to approach the great questions of life and reach the threshold where Truth abides, requires examination, contemplation, self-questioning, and ultimately self-awareness. No other way will lead you to self-actualization and Self realization. Ultimately, what holds us back is only our self-created obstacles and the generic ignorance of the mind that has forgotten its true nature and its Source. Freedom and the capacity to love all and forgive all are not accessible while the mind is running to a great extent on automatic, and controlled by unexamined egoic defense mechanisms. Defense of the person and the belief system is so ingrained in the human mind that it is very difficult to go beyond it and see clearly. When defenses are aroused consciously or unconsciously, clarity is lost and repetition of the past takes its place.

Observe your behavior and responses in certain situations over time and it will become self-evident how they repeat themselves over and over again. Developing self-awareness is a lengthy process that requires real interest and discipline. Being present in your mind and aware of its workings, the constant parade of thoughts, feelings, and impulses, is the fundamental practice that will lead you to self-understanding. The mind must be seen as it is, in action every day. Perseverance, courage, and self-honesty will bear fruit in the form of clarity. As the mind is busy all day, every day, so must the awareness of, the witnessing of the constant movement of mind be continued every day, all day.

Let the day be new
The old stay behind.
Every day sufficient in itself.
No need to fear what
Will come. The future will
Be what it is. Time is
Heedless of desires and wishes.
The river goes where it wills
No matter what it carries.
Anxiety and worry affect
Nothing but your own peace
Of mind. Recognize your place
In the Great Plan, leave all fear
With yesterday. Today is for
Living, die to yesterday
And come alive today.
You need not plan or defend
Against what cannot be avoided.
Do not fight the river.
The flow of life has its own
Logic and purpose. The way
Of the world has neither.
Be as a leaf on the tree
Of life. The seasons come
And go, the wind blows,
There is much movement and sound.

Leaves dancing back and forth
Yet they remain part of the tree.
When the time to let go comes
The leaf falls gently to the earth
And life goes on.

Reason is not something that seems to come easily to human thinking. Many of us probably believe that we are "reasonable" people, that our lives are based on beliefs and conclusions arrived at through a process of thinking guided by reason. To a certain extent, this is probably true, yet I suspect the range of our thinking and believing that rests on reason as its base is often grossly overestimated. In our modern era we could certainly use someone like Socrates, the ancient Greek philosopher, to call into question much of the belief system of modernity including the ideas of good and bad, and the idolatry of technological progress with its accompanying Western model of unlimited and unrestrained economic development as one size fits all.

If I were Socrates, I would probably begin by questioning what exactly do we mean when we speak of good in relation to human life? He would probably take the conversation down to the most fundamental meaning of the word good. What is good in relation to the individual and what is good in relation to society as a whole; is the answer the same in both cases? Is it possible to ascertain what is good for an individual independent of his/her membership in society? As humans are in general embedded in, are part of a societal framework of some kind and have been since the beginning of recorded history, I would say the most reasonable approach to understanding what is good for the individual is not to divorce it from the good of society as a whole. Our legal system with its checks and balances attempts, as a fundamental principle of law, to give maximum freedom to the individual without infringing on the freedom or well-being of another individual or group of individuals or society as a whole. Thus is the good or well-being of an individual not defined legally except in relation to society. This fundamental principle is unfortunately compromised where money and power are concerned in the direction of favoring those with money and power over those who have neither.

Let's continue by trying to reach a conclusion, a definition of what is meant by the term good in relation to human life. Ask ten people what the word means to them in that context and you will probably get ten different answers. In the interest of minimizing chaos and not getting lost in the wilderness of many different even contradictory opinions, I think it best to aim at a kind of fundamental and universal idea of good that theoretically applies to all beneath the level of individual differences and biases; at the least, we will try to get as close as possible to such a universal understanding. Inherent in thinking itself, in the use of language and concepts, are certain limitations that cannot be escaped, but we will do our best. Sometimes I think that all or at least much of Western philosophy arises from the attempt to understand or transcend these limitations, with each attempt coming from a different angle or starting point.

Human good must reasonably include the idea of physical well-being; i.e. food, shelter, and clothing in adequate supply, freedom from physical threat to life and limb, and in our present era, a means of earning the necessities of life which usually takes the form of a job or a business. And hopefully the job or business is fulfilling to the individual rather than being drudgery or outright unpleasant. To all this can be added access to healthcare when needed. It seems the idea of human good must then, for starters, include the fulfillment of basic physical needs. This much is clear.

Now comes the question of the inner life. Regarding the outer life of human beings there would be, I think, general agreement on the conclusions we have reached. That is the easy part. Modern Western society through its governmental programs and economic policies has and does attempt to satisfy the basic human needs of most of its citizens. This has been a huge and ongoing challenge given the vagaries of life, but one that has been met reasonably successfully for now. What is an even more difficult challenge and, it seems, is not being very successfully met by the modern version of human society is the satisfaction of the needs of our inner life.

Now, one could say that the responsibility for a condition of inner fulfillment rests with individuals themselves and I would agree. Yet is it a fact that outer circumstances and conditions exert much pressure on the inner life and can greatly affect its nature and stability. What is of special importance in this regard are the prevalent belief systems about the nature of reality, the nature of the individual, the purpose or meaning of life, as well as the effect on society and the individual of all the possibilities of human behavior and expression that are allowed and even encouraged.

There is at present in our Western civilization much emphasis on the rights of the individual to the point of extreme permissiveness in the sense of morals and behavior and, in consequence, the development of a way of life, a "lifestyle," that is based on hedonism, extreme self-centeredness, and a lack of a sense of responsibility towards others or society itself. We see the results of this way of living everywhere: drug and alcohol abuse, breakdown of the family, depression, suicide, mental illness, and the refusal to accept responsibility for our actions both individually and most tellingly in the business world and in political life. I would add here the endemic dishonesty that is constantly on display in the political sphere, and the organized and very lucrative practice of dishonesty in advertising. Not that dishonesty has not always been a part of human life in the public sphere, yet it seems to have been developed into a high art in our modern era and, as it is constantly on display before us through the media, this constant disregard for what is true as both policy and practice cannot but affect the human mind.

From studies that have been done by the social sciences, there is empirical evidence that a healthy family life and a sense of purpose for life affects human beings very positively and supports the development of an inner state of happiness and well-being. A state of happiness, contentment, a sense of emotional well-being, an attitude of helpfulness, tolerance, and kindness to others and a feeling of confidence and inner strength; all this would, I think, qualify as the condition of human good in the inner sense. Minds who function from this experience and feeling of life are the most likely to be responsible and supportive towards others and society as a whole. What contributes to this positive and helpful state of mind contributes to the human good, and what mitigates against it, obstructs or makes more difficult the attainment of this condition, does not contribute to the human good.

Following one's own self-centered desires, devotion to personal goals and accomplishments exclusively, as so many of us seem to be doing, may be temporarily sufficient to provide a kind of superficial condition of apparent "happiness." This "happiness," however, is dependent on keeping busy, staying in motion. If confronted with a period of time with nothing to do, no distraction or escape, the superficial happiness dissolves into the great emptiness within, which is then avoided by renewing the search for distraction. A happiness dependent on external factors and so easily lost is not real happiness. A state of constant excitement or busyness is not happiness, nor does it lead to self-fulfillment.

It's midafternoon on a late autumn day, lazy white clouds floating in a pale blue sky. The light is gentle and diffuse. The desert seems relaxed, almost as if asleep, and grateful for the cooler weather and the end of the harsh, bright summer sun. Some of its inhabitants are sleeping already, others will continue to move about all through the winter, absorbed in the endless search for food. The desert is not an easy place to live, yet there are many creatures who make it their home. No rain has fallen for the last two months; the mesquite and acacia trees and the many different bushes wait patiently, the grasses are dead. They will have to wait till spring or summer before they can live again. The desert plant life is patient and long-suffering. They know the rains will return so they wait, they wait. Nothing can be hurried where Mother Nature is concerned; all things have their seasons and follow their own rhythm. Even human life has its stages, its processes and patterns, from the life of the embryo to birth, childhood, adulthood, and eventually old age. We do not stand separate from or beyond the natural unfoldment of life; though in the midst of the artificiality of modern society, that fact is often forgotten.

It's easy to forget
From where we come
And who we depend upon.
Nature speaks with many voices
We have forgotten her language.
Increasingly the voices grow silent
If they are not heard.
The peoples of the earth
The old ones, are not listened to.
Ignored, shut away on their
Reservations, they too refuse
To speak. The Mother of us all
Forgives our ingratitude
Our indifference and carelessness,
Our hatred and arrogance.
When will we forgive ourselves
For what we have done?
When it's too late, when we
No longer care, who will speak

For us? Civilizations come and go.
We stand on the bones
Of those who came before us.
Their words live in our minds
Their genius is the foundation
Of how we live. Do we honor
The gifts they left us?

To avoid the present while chasing
Always the uncertain future
Is madness. Forgetting the
Harsh yet important lessons
Of the past is insanity.
Life reduced to public
Hypocrisy and deception,
To private isolation and greed
Economic development without conscience
Will lead to disaster. Mother Earth
Is not our playground, not
Our garbage dump. She is
Our home. To respect our home
Is simple reason, to not foul
Our nest is common sense.
It seems somewhere back in time
Society decided to take leave of its senses.

Destroy the earth beneath your feet
You will have nowhere to stand.
Poison the rivers and the oceans,
The fish and the garbage
Will lay stinking on our shores.
Never is there enough money
For those who worship greed.
The false idols with feet of clay

Will fall and we will
Go down with them.
Those who build their fortunes
On death will fall on their
Own swords. There is no free lunch
Dinner is not free either.
Take and take and take
As we have done, cannot
Go on forever. The bill will
Come due and we all will have
To pay it. There is no
Escaping the law of karma.
As we sow, so shall we reap.
The illusion of control cannot
Hide this fact forever.
The passage of time only
Delays the reckoning, the unavoidable.
Time is growing short
The day is almost over.
Our sun is about to sink beneath
The horizon of deliberate ignorance.
What is denied is always with us
Waiting for its turn.

What is reason? To reason is to think carefully, even logically, and consider all relevant factors in coming to a conclusion that is appropriate. So far so good. Yet to reason or be reasonable is often defined differently from person to person and society to society, at times even varying from one segment of society to another.

What does it mean to think carefully about anything? Thinking always involves valuations of good or bad, interpretations etc.; and this varies greatly from person to person. There are two sides to every issue as is obviously the case in our political life.

Generally both sides have a "reasoned argument" to support their case yet come to opposite conclusions. Why? Each side emphasizes to some degree certain facts and downplays or ignores others and it is this process and exclusion or inclusion of facts that results in opposite conclusions despite using "careful reasoning." One could say then that it is the assumptions and judgments on which evaluations are based that drive the use of reason. So the question arises: were these assumptions based on reason? So often are our assumptions a matter of bias or opinion, having little to do with reason.

It is extremely difficult to eliminate bias in human thinking. Yet a bias itself is not necessarily bad if it has a relationship to fact, is positive, and supports goodwill towards each other and a commitment to human good. There are many biases that do not meet these criteria and some that do. A bias arising from fear or hatred will obviously not support the authentic use of reason and will most likely sow discord rather than concord. A bias based on love and consideration of the rights and needs of others will possibly serve to bring us together. "Reasonable" people, I will be so bold as to say here, can generally be characterized by a thinking process, a use of reason, that is not dominated by fear and negative emotion.

Alone in the dark night
Harsh glare of streetlight and neon
What is felt by the strangers
Who walk beside us?
Do they love their children?
Do they fear the uncertainties of life
What the future may bring?
Are they so different from us
Or do we share the same mind
The same heart, the human heart?
Various sizes, shapes, and colors

The outer is just veneer.
Scratch the skin, we all bleed
The same color red. Our tears
And pain are one. In suffering
We are one family, one people.
The one Life lives Itself
Through everyone, all are related
There are no strangers here.

Our Mother Earth feeds us all.
Rain and snow fall on you
And on me. Sadness will visit
Every life. Laughter and joy
Will brighten every face.
The Creator loves His children
Without exception. Kindness to
Each other is our gift to Him.

Epilogue

The future is unknown, hidden behind the smokescreen of current events, obscured by our fear and denial. Current actions will have future consequences, that much is clear. Anticipating the consequences is where our human knowledge fails. Despite the aura of confidence and certainty that is part of the modern mindset, the potential chaos and uncertainty of life persists. It's true there is a huge modern global economic system based on powerful technology and the hard and skillful work of literally billions of people that produces a staggering amount of the necessities of life as well as a never-ending stream of new products. To the casual observer, this great and powerful beast we call modern society with its technology and endless production of goodies looks invincible and unstoppable. Like a huge beast stalking across the face of the earth, it gobbles up resources at an ever-increasing rate, devours entire forests; it is this fact that will be its undoing. Nothing, no process that is so greatly destructive, so insatiable, can go on indefinitely.

Our life is greatly affected by the instability of our human minds, our fears, our grievances, the distortions of our thinking processes, and our willful ignorance. Our clarity, our good and positive intentions, and our love for one another, result in good decisions with beneficial results for all. Too often, however, bias, selfishness, and fear in its many forms affect or direct our choices leading to unfortunate results. The greed that dominates the economic sphere has always been part of business activity. In our present situation, due to the size of business entities such as corporations and the power of modern technology, the effect of greed in action has an effect on the entire planet that is devastating. We as rabid consumers share responsibility for the damage. While it is true that the mass consumption way of life was invented and imprinted on the minds of the masses as a manipulation to both control them and create wealth for those who hold the reins of economic power, the decision to accept this way of life is individual; and we are complicit in the consequences of our economic system because of our decisions to be active and enthusiastic participants and the benefits we have received.

While it cannot be denied that living standards for many have improved during the modern age, and more importantly, human suffering due to disease and natural disasters has been greatly reduced and mitigated (and that is a very good thing!), along with this material improvement in the conditions of life have come new stresses and problems that negatively impact life and human happiness. These new factors are not going away anytime soon but rather seem to be intensifying along with their effects on the human mind.

Our modern society resembles nothing so much as the great ship Titanic with its huge size, its great forward momentum, and a very small rudder that cannot turn it in time to avoid what lies dead ahead. And like the passengers on that doomed ship of long ago, we are focusing too much of our time and energy on small meaningless activities such as playing shuffleboard or reading and rereading the lunch menu. No one on the great ship was expecting disaster; indeed the claim was made at the time that it was unsinkable. I observe the same naïve arrogance presently as prevailed regarding the Titanic, only today it is widespread and all pervasive. We are in danger, all of us, and few are willing to honestly consider our total situation or willing to support a complete change of course. Denial is the order of the day. I hope that all those who are willing to think for themselves and look at the big picture are also willing to examine their own mind and heart and commit to being exemplars of all-inclusive love and helpful to all.

SPIRITUALITY

O is a symbol of the world, of oneness and unity; this eye represents knowledge and insight. We publish titles on general spirituality and living a spiritual life. We aim to inform and help you on your own journey in this life.

If you have enjoyed this book, why not tell other readers by posting a review on your preferred book site? Recent bestsellers from O-Books are:

Heart of Tantric Sex
Diana Richardson
Revealing Eastern secrets of deep love and intimacy to Western couples.
Paperback: 978-1-90381-637-0 ebook: 978-1-84694-637-0

Crystal Prescriptions
The A-Z guide to over 1,200 symptoms and their healing crystals
Judy Hall
The first in the popular series of six books, this handy little guide is packed as tight as a pill-bottle with crystal remedies for ailments.
Paperback: 978-1-90504-740-6 ebook: 978-1-84694-629-5

Rising in Love

My Wild and Crazy Ride to Here and Now, with Amma, the
Hugging Saint

Ram Das Batchelder

Rising in Love conveys an author's extraordinary journey of
spiritual awakening with the Guru, Amma.

Paperback: 978-1-78279-687-9 ebook: 978-1-78279-686-2

Thinker's Guide to God

Peter Vardy

An introduction to key issues in the philosophy of religion.

Paperback: 978-1-90381-622-6

Your Simple Path

Find happiness in every step

Ian Tucker

A guide to helping us reconnect with what is really important in
our lives.

Paperback: 978-1-78279-349-6 ebook: 978-1-78279-348-9

365 Days of Wisdom

Daily Messages To Inspire You Through The Year

Dadi Janki

Daily messages which cool the mind, warm the heart and guide
you along your journey.

Paperback: 978-1-84694-863-3 ebook: 978-1-84694-864-0

Body of Wisdom

Women's Spiritual Power and How it Serves

Hilary Hart

Bringing together the dreams and experiences of women across
the world with today's most visionary spiritual teachers.

Paperback: 978-1-78099-696-7 ebook: 978-1-78099-695-0

Dying to Be Free
From Enforced Secrecy to Near Death to True Transformation
Hannah Robinson
After an unexpected accident and near-death experience, Hannah
Robinson found herself radically transforming her life, while a
remarkable new insight altered her relationship with her father, a
practising Catholic priest.
Paperback: 978-1-78535-254-6 ebook: 978-1-78535-255-3

The Ecology of the Soul
A Manual of Peace, Power and Personal Growth for Real People
in the Real World
Aidan Walker
Balance your own inner Ecology of the Soul to regain your
natural state of peace, power and wellbeing.
Paperback: 978-1-78279-850-7 ebook: 978-1-78279-849-1

Not I, Not other than I
The Life and Teachings of Russel Williams
Steve Taylor, Russel Williams
The miraculous life and inspiring teachings of one of the World's
greatest living Sages.
Paperback: 978-1-78279-729-6 ebook: 978-1-78279-728-9

On the Other Side of Love
A Woman's Unconventional Journey Towards Wisdom
Muriel Maufroy
When life has lost all meaning, what do you do?
Paperback: 978-1-78535-281-2 ebook: 978-1-78535-282-9

Practicing A Course In Miracles
A Translation of the Workbook in Plain Language and With
Mentoring Notes
Elizabeth A. Cronkhite
The practical second and third volumes of The Plain-Language
A Course In Miracles.
Paperback: 978-1-84694-403-1 ebook: 978-1-78099-072-9

Quantum Bliss
The Quantum Mechanics of Happiness, Abundance, and Health
George S. Mentz
Quantum Bliss is the breakthrough summary of success and
spirituality secrets that customers have been waiting for.
Paperback: 978-1-78535-203-4 ebook: 978-1-78535-204-1

The Upside Down Mountain
Mags MacKean
A must-read for anyone weary of chasing success and happiness
– one woman's inspirational journey swapping the uphill slog for
the downhill slope.
Paperback: 978-1-78535-171-6 ebook: 978-1-78535-172-3

Your Personal Tuning Fork
The Endocrine System
Deborah Bates
Discover your body's health secret, the endocrine system, and
'twang' your way to sustainable health!
Paperback: 978-1-84694-503-8 ebook: 978-1-78099-697-4

Readers of ebooks can buy or view any of these bestsellers by clicking on the live link in the title. Most titles are published in paperback and as an ebook. Paperbacks are available in traditional bookshops. Both print and ebook formats are available online.

Find more titles and sign up to our readers' newsletter at
http://www.johnhuntpublishing.com/mind-body-spirit

Follow us on Facebook at https://www.facebook.com/OBooks/
and Twitter at https://twitter.com/obooks

Printed and bound by PG in the USA